Un-dependently Yours: Imagining A World Beyond The Red Carpet

Experiments in Cinema
yearbook 2015

Edited by Bryan Konefsky with River Quane and David Camarena

A Basement Films Production

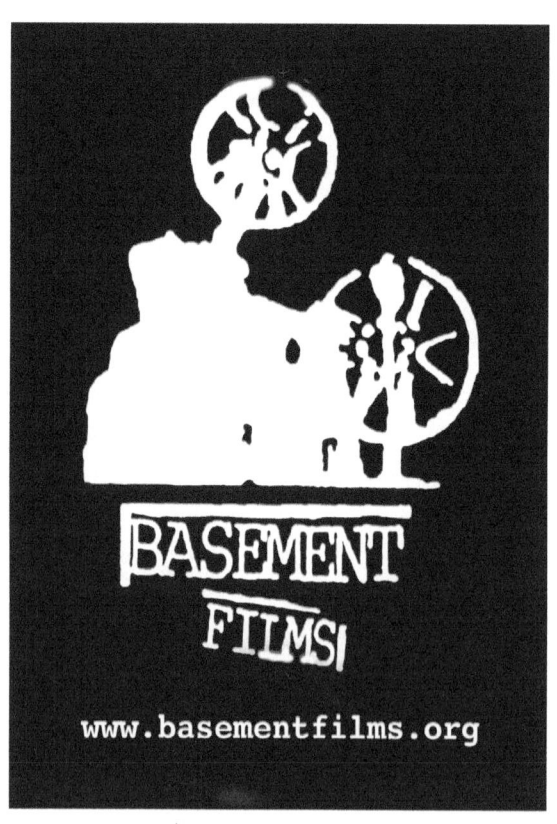

www.basementfilms.org

Un-dependently Yours: Imagining A World Beyond The Red Carpet

Experiments in Cinema
yearbook 2015

Publisher
Basement Films

Editors
Bryan Konefsky, River Quane and David Camarena

Layout
River Quane

Additional Brainstorming
Bryan Konefsky, River Quane, Michelle Mellor

Print Run
150

Basement Films
PO Box 9229
Albuquerque, New Mexico
USA 87119
www.basementfilms.org
www.experimentsincinema.org
basementfilms.av@gmail.com

Cover image
"May beats a carpet," 1927, Manitoba, Canada, photographer unknown.

ISBN 978-1-329-00513-6

Table of Contents

Acknowledgements:

This first (ever) "Experiments in Cinema" yearbook would not be possible without the amazing support of many, many, oh so many people. I am eternally grateful to have such a supportive partner in life, my dear Patti. Thanks for the thoughtful insistence (that this project is worthwhile) by my assistant director/tech director Michelle Mellor, and for the enthusiasm (and exacting attention to detail) of my editorial staff, River Quane and David Camarena. This project was inspired by the "Alternative Film/Video" festival's archive of published yearbooks shared by Greg de Cuir Jr, Milos Korac and Milan Milosaviljevic when Basement Films visited Belgrade. Additionally I would like to thank my parents Vic and Jeanne, David Nelson and Keif Henley (David founded Basement Films and Keif went on to nurture the organization into what it is today), Gerry Fialka whose "PXL This" festival was the first festival I ever attended, Chrisstina Hamilton, Bart Weiss and George Manupelli who encouraged me to "go for it" and realize my dream of producing "Experiments in Cinema." I would like to thank Mark Moscato from "My House Cinema" for coining the phrase "un-dependent cinema" (which I freely borrow). Special thanks to Susan Dever who found a way to carve a bit of time for me to imagine, Ruth Bradley who supported my own creative work way-back-when, and additional members of Basement Films whose passion for all-things-cinematic inspire me every single day: Beth Hansen, Senaida Garcia, Jenette Isaacson, Sahra Saedi, Peter Lisignoli, Asha Hopkins, Shawn Smith, Evan White and Britney King. Two former members of Basement Films also need to be mentioned as they have gone on to do remarkable work and keep the faith: Ben Popp and Marika Borgeson, you are the best! There are two people who I have been "in conversation with" for the last 25+ years and our ongoing dialogue is nothing less than priceless: thanks Gene Youngblood and Jean Luc Mayoussier! Most importantly I would like to thank everyone who participated in this volume for taking the time to share with us their writing and their thoughts. Finally, a heartfelt "thank you" to the audiences who have attended "Experiments in Cinema" through the years, and believed in our mission in spite or our "now and again" growing pains.

In conclusion, please allow me to share one of my absolute favorite quotes written by one of my absolute favorite people of all time:

"Great art has always gone to the masses, to their hopes and dreams, for that spark that kindled their souls. The rest, 'the many, all too many' as Nietzsche called mediocrity, have been mere commodities that can be bought with money, cheap glory, or social position."
- Emma Goldman

Bryan Konefsky
Founder/Director, Experiments in Cinema
El Presidente, Basement Films

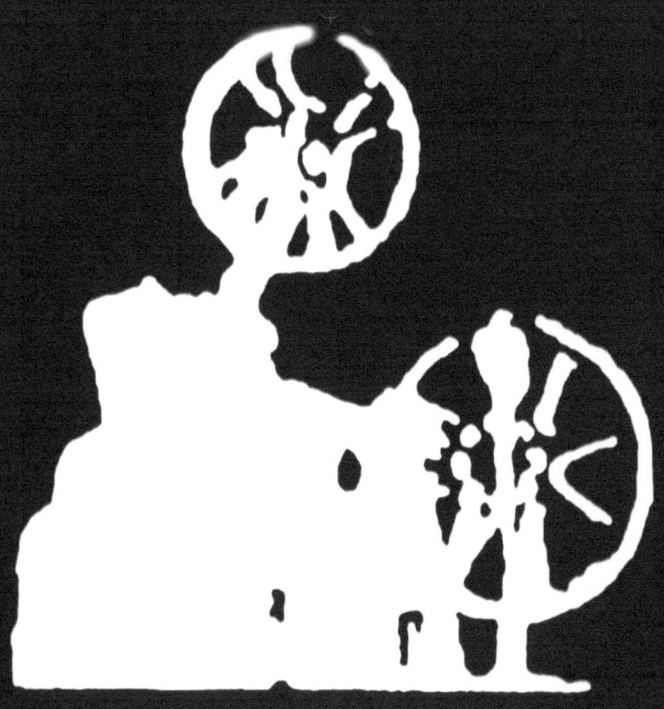

BASEMENT
FILMS

www.basementfilms.org

Introduction

By: Bryan Konefsky

The original title for this anthology was likely going to be "I Piss On Your Red Carpet." However, I am happy to report that I no longer feel the need for such "young, loud snotty-ness." As my mother used to tell me, "if you can't say anything nice then don't say anything at all."

After many years of participating in un-dependent film festivals, I challenged myself, and Basement Films, to craft an event that was mindful of the good, the bad and the ugly of those experiences. I imagined an international festival that was non-competitive, inclusive, inviting and always filmmaker-friendly. More than anything I hoped to create a micro-community of like-minded media artists (and enthusiasts) who might come together in dialogue around their particular perspectives of "the state of the art." Ten years later, Experiments in Cinema is happily celebrating its milestone 10th anniversary.

I believe it is our responsibility, as modern day traveling media-troubadours, to share with others our sense of the human condition from our individual corners of the world. This sharing necessitates thoughtful and protracted conversations, not industry-minded Q&A sessions. "Sharing" is an integral condition of being un-dependent.

Film artist Scott Stark once stated, "the art world doesn't understand us (un-dependents) and the film industry has no interest in us." Hence, we are free to live in an ecstatic state of "in-betweenness," knowing that for us fulfillment will manifest itself beyond the contemptuous and divisive trappings of capitalism. When the ills of competition and aesthetic ambulance chasing fall away, what emerges is an exhilarating sense of altruism, inventiveness and community.

So gentle reader, drink deep as you travel through this anthology of writing and remember how generous these authors have been sharing their thoughts and ideas about living a creative life in the context of the micro-communities we call film festivals. My hope is that by the end of your journey, you will be transformed and perhaps radicalized in terms of recognizing the value of your media voice and that it is your responsibility to participate in shaping future trends of cultural representation.

Full report to follow.

Bryan Konefsky
Founder/Director, Experiments in Cinema
El Presidente, Basement Films

Blown Off the Big Screen

By: Gene Youngblood

There was a time when the leading edge of cinema could be seen in theaters. But in the 1960s, explosive innovations in cinematic practice around the world blew the leading edge right off the commercial screen. Since then, the technological convergence of film and video has rendered distinctions between them arbitrary and confusing. So we change the way we talk: film and video become "the moving image" and experimental film and video come together on the "alternative screen," the site of nonindustrial, non-commercial practice in the moving image.

The alternative screen is the fine arts and intellectual tradition in the movies. It's where we now track the leading edge of moving image practice, both cultural and technological. It's where we see the most radical and inventive movies ever made, movies that spring from artistic, cultural, and political desire, with monetary reward and popularity being secondary or negligible concerns. Not commodities for mass consumption, they are the true independents.

Straight-ahead fictional narratives seldom appear on the alternative screen. Its prevalent practices are moving image equivalents of the personal and political essay, the diary, the portrait, the landscape, the lyric poem, the experimental narrative -- in other words, the languages of subjectivity and of social engagement, without which a culture is dead. These works are often demanding. They aren't entertainment any more than poetry or political discourse are. They don't necessarily explain themselves. They respect our intelligence. They assume our brains are somehow still alive, that we prefer to "read" the moving image, to interpret, imagine, and come to our own conclusions.

There is a long tradition of noncommercial practice in the moving image, but few people are familiar with it. While the other arts are celebrated for their highest achievements, cinema is not. The moving image is compromised in every culture. The most powerful and expressive of the arts (because it contains all of them), cinema is at the same time the most trivialized, identified almost exclusively with commodity culture and mass consumption. (In what other art do we find it so frequently necessary to caution that a work is "not for everyone" or that it might have a "limited audience"?)

If most people are unfamiliar with the alternative screen, it's because of capitalist hegemony over moving image production and distribution. The industrialization of cinema requires the mass media to legitimize "show business" and to de-legitimize alternative practices as not being "real movies." The result is severely limited distribution for movies that are "difficult to market," which means restricted public exposure to the alternative screen, which means limited desire for artistic and intellectual discourse in the most powerful communication medium in history.

This is not to say that the alternative screen is of no consequence in American culture. Genuine innovation always begins in the margins, and, precisely because of its marginality, the alternative screen has profoundly influenced not only mall movies but popular culture in general. Much of mainstream culture as we know it would not exist without Kenneth Anger, Andy Warhol, Bruce Conner, George Kuchar, and Jack Smith, visionary pioneers of cultural reflexivity in the cinema. Yet how many people who profess to love movies have sought out their films?

To some extent, video distribution democratizes access to the alternative screen for both makers and audience. One can rent for the same price a film that cost $20 million to make and one that cost twenty dollars (a George Kuchar diary, say, funnier than anything Hollywood is capable of imagining). This is encouraging, but distribution doesn't equal recognition. There's no saturation advertising to cultivate desire for the alternative screen and familiarize us with its creations. Nothing sells; everything is sold, and we don't choose a dish we haven't been made to want. In spite of this, more moving image artists are producing more films and videos today than ever before, and more is being written about the alternative screen today than in any previous period.

Five programs in this year's festival represent Taos Talking Pictures' commitment to the alternative screen (see sidebar). In subsequent festivals we hope to expand our video programming, to reach out internationally for the latest practices from other cultures, and to include video installations and works in interactive multimedia. What's important, however, is not the medium but the artistic, cultural, and political practices a medium makes possible. What's important is the voice of the Other, speaking the languages of poetic vision or political engagement. What's important is the expressive potential of the moving image in any and all of its technological and cultural forms. What can a movie be and do, and who can we be as spectators who come to different screens for different reasons? That is the value of festivals such as ours: to present a broad spectrum of projects and possibilities, modes of cinematic being.

_____

About the Author

Gene Youngblood is a theorist of media arts and politics, and a respected scholar in the history and theory of alternative cinemas. His best known book, *Expanded Cinema*, was the first to consider video as an art form and has been credited with helping to legitimate the fields of computer art and media arts. He is also known for his pioneering work in the media democracy movement, a subject on which he has taught, written, and lectured since 1967.

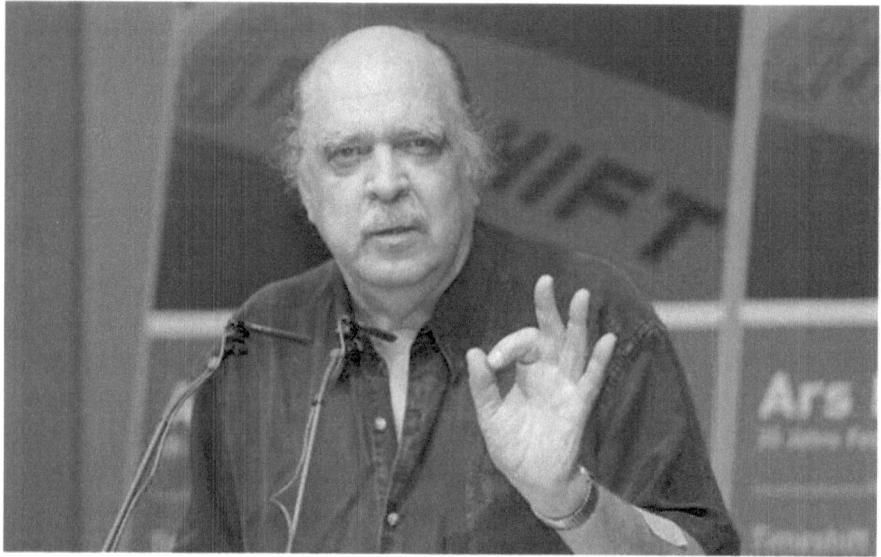

Portrait of Gene Youngblood

We Sit in the Dark (Safety in Numbers)

By: Sasha Waters Freyer

Film festivals are pageants at which every sin of the Seven Deadly (but for Sloth, we are working here, people!) is on Parade—Lust, Gluttony, Greed, Wrath, Envy, and Pride. Here we convene as friends, rivals, muses, mentors, ex-students, ex-teachers, ex-lovers, acolytes, and Art Stars to share recognition and sometimes failure, conversation, and community. Our lives unfold year after year, stitched into certain moments in festival time and space – this year in New Mexico, another in New York, that time in Ohio. Sitting in the dark or at the bar, we are woven into a web as disparate and mutual as a small galaxy.

We create, we mine our silver, suffer disappointment; we find inspiration and one another in the most unexpected places.

1. We sit in the dark, it is the world premiere of E's film, my former student, now friend. I have seen this short before—a funny, formally inventive and beautiful experiment in cinema. Later in the week it will deserve and win an impressive award. I squeeze E's shoulder, hard. Screening at this festival has been his unspoken dream for years. Ambitious E. As a student, he was haughty, impatient with his peers—no time for navel-gazing, self-indulgence or sentiment! Smoke and mirrors to mask his sweet and broken heart, I think. I squeeze his arm again. I squeeze back tears to watch this heart crack open on screen.

2. We sit in the dark, whispering before the projector hums into action. I need to hire a filmmaker to teach next year. You rave about her and she seems perfect. Only later will I discover the Old News to Most that you slept with her when she was your student.

3. We sit in the dark, G., age seven months, snuggled tight against me. The Michigan Theater is huge, packed! This may not fly—a baby at a screening. G.wriggles but remains calm as the program unspools, one short film after the next. Now a brand new, exquisite work by Nathaniel Dorsky. Luscious. Silent. G. seizes the moment, fills the auditory void MAMA!!! MAMA!!! We are politely, firmly, instructed to leave.

4. We sit at the bar—there is James Franco, two empty bar stools over! Later, I will wish I had asked him, If a Hollywood movie were being made about this night, who would you want to play you? But even weak wit fails me now, it's almost 2am. This is Not the Kind of Festival where I can openly or sneakily snap a photo of him, dammit. I am in an epic fight with my sister, N., we haven't spoken in months. Despite the hour, I text her OMG I'm sitting next to James Franco!!!! Ha.

5. We sit in the dark. My new short film is screening in New York before a wacky 1970s cult film. D. is a PBS-style documentarian—old school. I don't know how much he goes in for experimental or cult films, but he is game. My very first paid production job was with D., back in 1993. He interviewed me with his dirty-socked feet propped up on his desk as noisy Ninth Avenue whirred below his office window. Now he is here with me as an old friend and I am grateful.

6. We sit the dark, J. is hyper sensitive to visual over-stimulation. He leaves mid-screening while I stay to watch the whole program of pulsing, underground film abstractions. At the bar, J. tells the dude sitting next to him Experimental film makes me want to throw up. Said dude, unbeknownst to J., is the festival founder and long-time programmer. He laughs and says That will be our motto for next year!

We Sit in the Dark (Safety in Numbers)

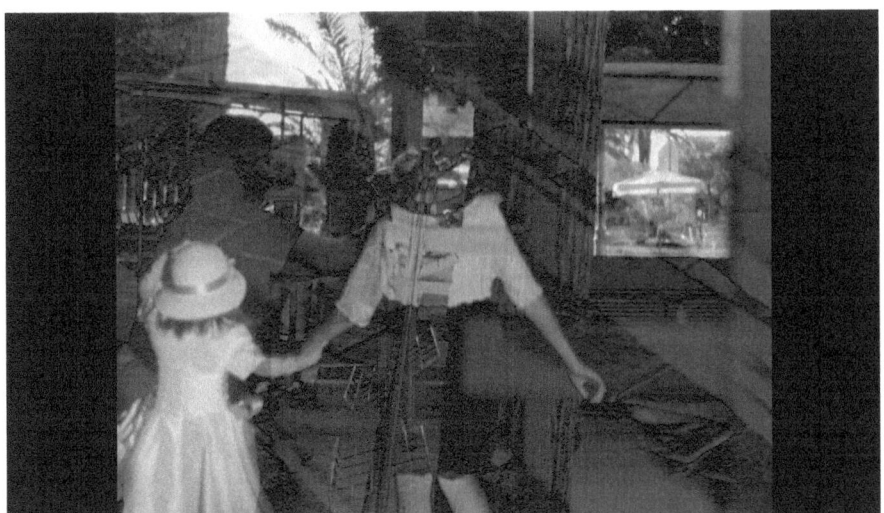

Still from *Garden Stone* (2015) By Sasha Waters Freyer

7. We sit at the bar and you uncharacteristically order soda. In the hotel that night, you tell me you are pregnant with your third child, due shortly before your 46th birthday. It's a secret, you say, it was an accident. Before I can stop myself I blurt, Why aren't you having an abortion? Another child at our age seems dangerous, crazy. You are appalled by my question. We have been friends for so very long, you soon forgive me. Still, I am sorry I said that.

8. I sit in the dark, surrounded by friends and strangers who seem utterly engrossed in this film. Exhausted by my unraveling home life, emotionally isolated, I can't focus. I was supposed to spend five days here, but I will stay a mere 24 hours because I am so worried about J. He is in a crisis, losing it, very sick; I am both relieved and scared to be away from him. I lie to almost everyone I know here, tell them I am leaving early for an unrelated reason. Thank God for D. who understands the truth and comes to visit soon after. He is the help for which I did not know how to ask.

9. We sit at the bar, laughing with the festival pals we have come to know over years of screenings and late nights like this

one. There is F., who calls out "bub" or "lurker" to all, and B., whose prickly arrogance belies a deeper affability. There's T. who, it surprises me to learn, has quite the rep for sleeping with much younger women—he seems so modest, unassuming. Also, he is married. There is S. Now, she is just a bitch. Why so unfriendly though we have met several times and know so many people in common?

10. We sit in the dark, my new film is premiering! The lab sent the 16mm print directly here—I've never seen it projected. Twenty seconds in, a thin blue line dances across the screen. Wiggling and jiggling and blue on the black-and-white image—a scratch! My new print is scratched and I will have to ask the festival to replace it and that conversation could be Very Awkward. They might claim the scratch is Not Their Fault. The projector stutters, starts and stops – starts again. Suddenly it grinds to a halt and the image on screen freezes, bubbles and melts. Four hundred people collectively gasp: Ohhhhhh!!!! The film is on fire, burned in the gate. It is a terrible moment made easier by knowing the huge roomful of fellow filmmakers and celluloid lovers sympathetically share my shock and pain. Also: the ruined print will be replaced after all. OBVIOUSLY.

11. We sit in the dark. L's new film is a miracle. Brilliant, truly. I have admired her personally—her generosity and kind insights, her capacious embrace of community and parenting and artistic production, her ever-present smile!—since she was my teacher. But to be perfectly honest, I've had mixed feelings about her films in the past. They seemed Too Disparate formally and in the scope of their concerns. Now I see she was and is the perfect mentor – exploratory, risk-taking, not bound by strict categories of cinema or art or documentary. And she is always, always making work.

12. We sit outside smoking, while inside our old friends, our families, watch the film that features you. You were very sick during those two years of on-and-off shooting. Although you are

better now, it is hard for both of us—especially together and in person—to hear those unhinged messages you left on my phone, to remember the scary upheaval that was your life then, including hospital stays and time in jail. It was brave of you to let me keep it all in the film, to be here tonight in front of all these people – those who know you and will understand, and those who don't.

13. We sit in the dark, G. and R., and my mother. I love to share this festival with them, although most of the films are not of interest to children. They travel with me for the hotel pool and Special Family Time when I am not attending screenings. But today there is an imaginative and awesome film about basketball! What's not to love?

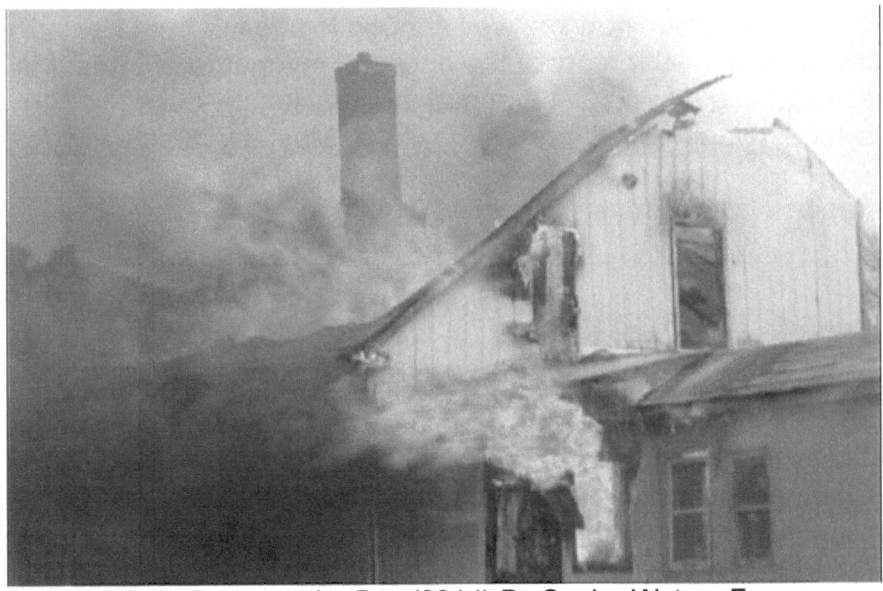

Still from *Burn out the Day* (2014) By Sasha Waters Freyer

14. We sit in the dark at the Siskel Center in Chicago, two days before Election Day 2008. Barack Obama is about to become our first African-American President. The air inside the theater and on the streets is electric. We know. He will win! It's going to happen! A strong, invisible filigree of joy binds us all, across the

city. Massive smiles and high fives everywhere. Looking back, I try to hang on to that feeling – before the disappointment, the confusion, our deflated realities.

15. We sit in the dark, I was surprised to run into you here, and nervous about you seeing my film. In the past you've made it clear that you are—well, ambivalent, would be a nice way to say it—not interested in my work. Our relationship has been strange and tense across the years. You are the only person about whom I use the word "frenemy," and I laugh when I do, but I think it's apt. Two Scorpios who excel in smoke and mirrors—always cool professionals in public (admittedly, you more than me). Our former students would be stunned to discover how we sometimes raged at each other. The tears and curses. Hurt accusations followed by long stretches of bitter silence. But you know me well enough to see the truth behind this new film – the story of the house of my marriage burned to ashes. I'm glad you Get It and at the very least—out of sympathy perhaps?—pretend to like it. Maybe you actually do.

Sasha Waters Freyer, October 2014

About the Author

Sasha Waters Freyer is a moving image artist trained in photography and film whose features and shorts have screened widely in the U.S. and abroad, including on the Sundance Channel, the Telluride, Tribeca and Rotterdam Film Festivals, L.A. Film Forum and the Film Society of Lincoln Center, and have been reviewed in *Variety, The New Yorker* and *ArtForum*. She is the Chair of the Department of Photography & Film at Virginia Commonwealth University, the number one public college of art in the U.S.

FLEXfest and the (Past and) Future of Festivals

By: Roger Beebe

As I sit down to write this, I've just handed off the reins of FLEXfest after a decade in the saddle (That's how the metaphor lines up, right? Reins/saddle? It felt like a bucking bronco for most of that decade, not a stagecoach or prairie schooner.) Having just stepped away from the festival has both perils and possibilities for these musings, allowing me perhaps the perspective of some (small) distance from the festival, but also perhaps colored by the nostalgia for the world I've left behind.

When I moved to Gainesville, Florida, FLEXfest's home base, in 2000, I'd been running a festival in Chapel Hill, North Carolina for a few years. That festival, Flicker, had been started by Norwood Cheek as a place for locals to show their small-gauge (mostly super 8) films every two months. Flicker was a unique festival at a unique time, and when I moved to Florida, I had some idea about trying to recreate its special magic, but that idea never turned into action.

Four years into my Gainesville stay, though, I was really starting to feel the limitations of the city's cultural offerings, and so in a somewhat frenzied few months, I committed to trying to add to those offerings by both starting a film festival and opening a video store. For the former, I recruited a crew of pretty amazing students (including now-accomplished filmmakers Jodie Mack and Charlotte Taylor), and we sprang into action. None of us knew exactly what we were doing, but I figured I'd been to enough festivals that we could make it work.

The model that I had in mind from the outset was a combination of year-round local events (which would just be FLEX) and then an annual international short film & video festival (FLEXfest, a subtle distinction in nomenclature that may not have been especially clear to anyone). The first events that we did doubled as fundraisers for the festival, since we didn't have any other funding in place. Our most regular events were outdoor screenings of 16mm features from our archive (Cinema under the Stars, or C.u.t.S.). We also held a local film and music event (a "FLEXtravaganza") in a clearing in a bamboo forest with a giant screen made of a patchwork of whitewashed cardboard boxes that Jodie stitched together. These events mostly proved to be pretty popular, and while we didn't raise thousands of dollars, we did raise hundreds while also raising awareness (and a little Hell too). We did fill the coffers with some money from entry fees as well, but at a modest $10 a pop for domestic entrants, we're again not talking about thousands of dollars. (With about 125 entries that first year, many of which came from abroad—so exempted from entry fees—you can see how the math works out.)

So, we had a little money. I had some projectors. Sound...was a work in progress. (We bought a stereo receiver, which ended up getting fried about halfway through the fest. We were able to return it, and we got a lot better at audio in the years that followed.) Our venues were mostly free (the WARPHaus, a gallery/studio owned by the Art Department) or just took a cut of the door (the Ark, a legendary, now-defunct Gainesville punk venue). We paid a little for the one venue that could present 35mm (the Hippodrome Theater, which has since sadly dumped its 35mm projector), and we may have paid something modest for our opening night venue as well (the Thomas Center, a building owned by the City of Gainesville that we later would use regularly for Cinema under the Stars). We paid for plane tickets for our two jurors, Naomi Uman and Tony Gault, and they (along with our other guests—among them Rob Todd and Lisa Marr) were put up in my house, which we called the FLEX Hotel for the duration of the fest. But most of our operating budget (including what we took in at the door—probably our biggest source of funds) we ended up giving out as prizes to the winning filmmakers.

The festival was enough of a success—solid attendance, interesting films, etc.—that we decided to do it again. It was enough of a Herculean labor, though, that I insisted on a different structure for the second year. Unlike most festivals, we (or I?) decided that the competitive FLEXfest would be a biennial event with a curated or invitational affair in the off years. What this meant was that we'd invite a small group of filmmakers to come to Gainesville and present two programs each: one, a program of their films; the other, a program of work that influenced them. This seemed like a good way to get some older work screened in town (since the competitive festival only allowed us to screen work made in the last few years) and it allowed us to feature full bodies of work by interesting makers—Bill Brown, Scott Stark, and Deborah Stratman in year two—but at its core, the decision was motivated by my/our exhaustion at the end of the first year. The festival staff was (and has remained) all volunteer, so these were hours everyone was stealing from their other responsibilities.

The rest, as they say, is history. The festival grew, doubling the number of entries for each competitive festival, with somewhere north of 800 for the 2013 fest. We eventually got annual support through UF's Student Government funds (by establishing a student-run FLEX affiliate) in addition to semi-regular support from the University of Florida's Center for the Humanities in the Public Sphere for the curated festival (where we didn't have submission fees to provide a baseline of funding), and we purchased a small amount of necessary gear out of an equipment slush fund that I controlled through the Film & Media Studies Program. (Chief among the gear was a little mixing board and a pair of JBL EON speakers to address our sound woes.) Florida is last in the nation in per-capita arts spending—the figure is something like 75 cents per person per year—but we did get a $2500 grant in 2009 that allowed us to

Roger Beebe

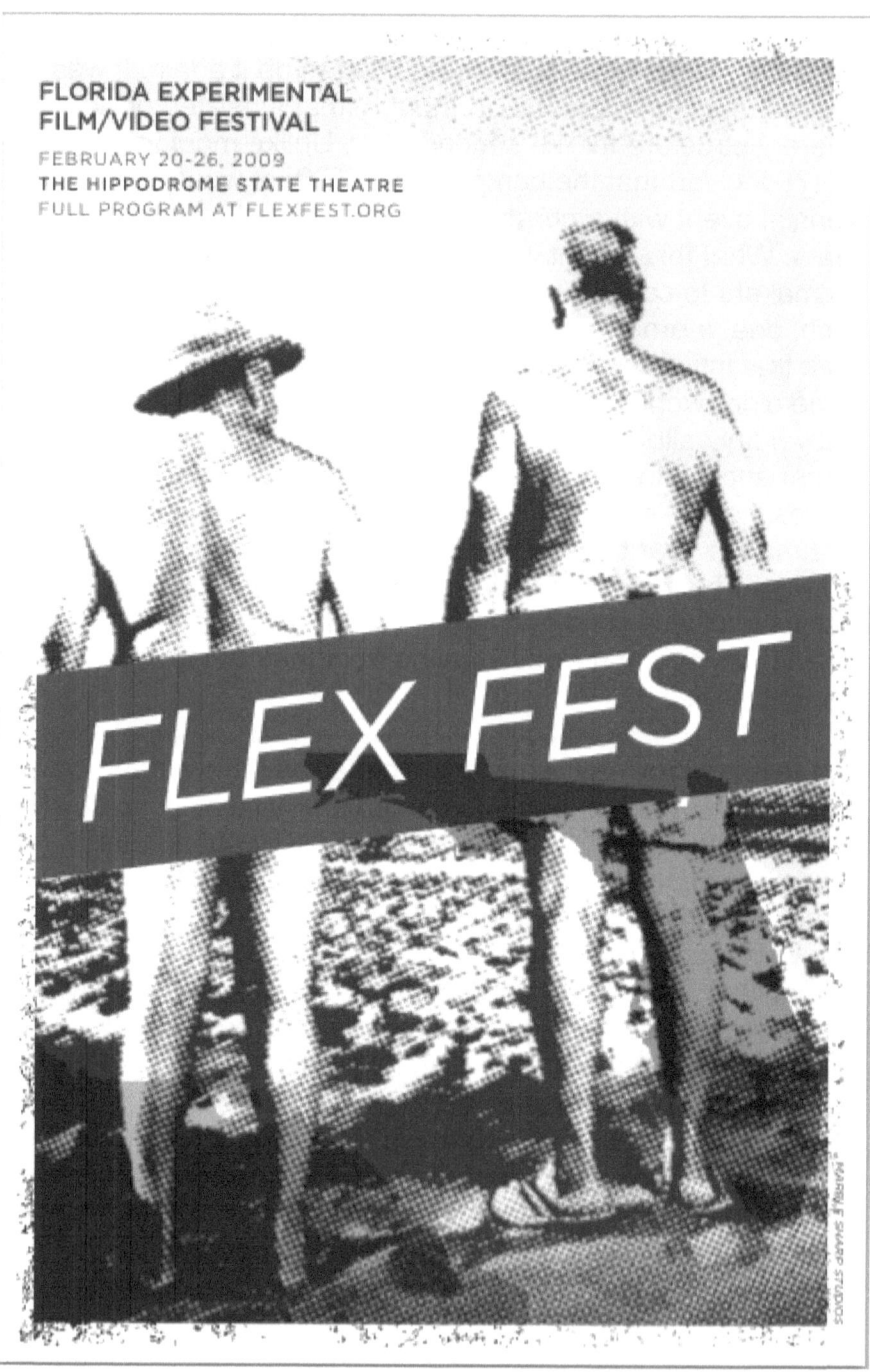

extend the festival to a full week instead of the three- or four-day weekend that it usually has run. We basically remained true to the model that we established those first years though as the festival grew, never quite becoming a grown-up, stable institution, despite, I think, becoming a fairly esteemed festival.

I threatened to quit after every festival—I knew the toll it took on my own filmmaking (and sleep!)—and even publicly announced my retirement more than once, in the hope that that'd finally force me to step away. But my clean break only came when I moved away in January 2015 to take a job in the Department of Art at Ohio State. (I'm not entirely joking when I say that I partially took the new job in order to run away from my responsibilities with the festival and video store!)

I was thinking back recently about all my favorite festivals that don't exist any longer—Cinematexas, PDX, NY Underground, THAW, MicroCineFest, etc.—and while I'm not writing a post mortem of FLEX (since I left it in Alisson Bittiker's able hands), I definitely now understand why festivals don't live forever. Especially in the U.S. where the funding situation is so precarious, a festival's survival really depends on the planets aligning perfectly. But just because these things don't last forever, it doesn't mean they didn't do anything. In fact, all those festivals I listed above changed me forever in ways both big and small. The kind of community that I feel is definitely a consequence of the connections I made at those festivals. Even my desire to keep making work was sustained in large part by the validation that those festivals gave me and my films. Sure, getting rejected by festivals can be a bummer too—and I know I was rejected over the years by more than one of those fests. And, sure, entry fees do add up, especially when you're first getting going and have both shallower pockets and more need to send your work out widely to fill your CV. But despite all that, there's really no substitute in the virtual world for the things that I got from festivals, and I know that when I put the good and bad on a scale, it's pretty heavily tipped in fests' favor.

About a decade ago, the short-time director of one of those aforementioned fests offered a bleak outlook for the future of such gatherings. He predicted that the price of jet fuel would continue to rise and that with the difficulty of post-9/11 travel, fewer and fewer people would want to make the trip to festivals, so the entire enterprise was doomed. It turns out he was wrong, at least as far as I can tell. I went to Ann Arbor last year (now a short drive from my new home in Columbus), and I was blown away by the number of makers who were there. And the pleasures of this mode of exhibition weren't only available to dinosaurs like me who're clinging to the culture of a previous era. The small group of students I brought to the festival with me were all ecstatic about their experience of the festival, and I expect that years down the road at least one of them will be in a position to reflect back on the way that trip changed his trajectory forever.

So while, yes, Vimeo, YouTube, etc. have provided other valuable ways of getting this work out into the world and while venues like Facebook allow people to remain connected without necessarily crossing paths in physical space, they're only supplements, not substitutes for what festivals still provide. Being in a big dark room with your devices turned off, surrounded by a crowd of your community (or by a crowd of strangers—that's amazing too), remains an experience like none other. It's also the experience of the films (and videos) that most makers imagine as they're laboring for hours (days, weeks) on those films. In the end, while it's true that the lights of experimental film festivals have never burned with the blinding intensity of the klieg lights of a Hollywood premiere, I suspect they'll keep burning with the reliable warmth of the 350-watt ELC lamps that power my classroom 16mm projectors. So three cheers for those who're keeping those projectors running, literally or figuratively.

(This is what I believe they call preaching to the choir, isn't it? If so, then CAN I GET AN "AMEN"?)

About the Author

Roger Beebe is an Associate Professor in the Department of Art at the Ohio State University. He has screened his films around the globe at such unlikely venues as the CBS Jumbotron in Times Square and McMurdo Station in Antarctica as well as more likely ones including Rotterdam, Sundance, and the Museum of Modern Art. Beebe is also a film programmer: he ran Flicker, a festival of small-gauge film in Chapel Hill, NC, from 1997-2000 and was the founder and Artistic Director of FLEX, the Florida Experimental Film Festival from 2004-2014.

Michael Betancourt

why
(notes on the White Cube—Black Box—Telescreen Triad)

By: Michael Betancourt

I have no idea how to write this essay, but it's not for a lack of things to say: I don't trust my easy answers. I see this notion 'cinema' simultaneously from several perspectives—maker, curator, historian, theorist—and so I require my answers to always have sources, their logic to be apparent. These answers don't have immediately obvious reasoning, yet they feel "obvious," arousing my suspicions—they come unbidden, without effort, giving me doubts about their origins: are these *my* answers, or are they simply internalized, remembered from elsewhere and mistaken for my own? Any answer that arrives instantly has this same problem—being known without having to think makes me suspicious. My investigation of reasons— known without being thought—are in consideration of the question:

Why care about "the black box" (and *experimental* festivals in particular)?

My answer begins with *of course* . . . and that is the problem. As an "experimental filmmaker" this question feels almost ridiculous to me, absurd even, since I don't consider or regard what I do as "film"—which is what makes me suspicious about the instant "of course." Yet I have this feeling *all* film festivals are essential, and those few festivals focused on *experimental* media even more so than those that address commercial production. This distinction between the commercial and experimental festival is especially important given the quantity of commercial venues generally, and the very real differences between commercial narrative motion pictures and experimental productions. It is fundamentally a matter of conception: commercial production focuses primarily on

why
(notes on the White Cube-Black Box-Telescreen Triad)

"feature-length" narratives, while experimental works tend to be shorter and conceived along entirely different aesthetics. Experimental movies are not "stepping stones," "calling cards" or other ephemera made before moving on to make "serious" commercial features. It is the *concerted* focus on those specific, inherent issues *other* than what happens in the narrow conventions of commercial narratives that is the point: to judge "experimental film" by the concerns of commercial narrative is to misunderstand the 'experimental' entirely. This field is uncoupled from the commercial marketplace, and so has the aesthetic freedom to develop cinematic *art* apart from the limited forms of commercial storytelling.

Distrust of my own immediate, unconsidered response is the real cause of my uncertainty about how to answer the question posed. We need *experimental* festivals precisely because they are one of the only moments where we *do* get to see groups of carefully chosen works shown together—and not as the small-scale experience of the telescreen, or under the vicissitudes of white cube (art gallery) *en passant* viewing—at large-scale, inside the 'black box' theater, in *the* projected form that historically is "cinema."

This historically-derived idea of "cinema" begins with a fact: motion pictures *are* different when projected at full scale, as big compositions playing out in ways utterly distinct from what we can see on the telescreen or in the unstructured watching of the art gallery: the pacing changes, montage, and framing have a difference valence. Scale matters, as does the programming of the show as a whole. These things distinguish the festival from the web video and the art installation. The real question here has to do with the nature of "cinema," the role of the experimental festival especially in creating this *thing*; what it entails when confronted by the alternatives—the white cube spaces coincident with the art gallery, and the peculiarly ungrounded viewing of the telescreen.

21

It is an important distinction. Our tendency to fall into divisions based on media, technology, and exhibition venue suggest differences that appear to be "givens." They are assumptions about the nature of our media and our relationships to whose ideological content is not subject to direct questioning precisely because these things are "givens." This label, *"experimental"* poses another immediate question, one the earlier question presupposes:

What is *Experimental* in 'Experimental Cinema'?

Historically, this label was first applied by Lewis Jacob's short-lived magazine, "Experimental Cinema," in the early 1930s—but knowing this information does little to illuminate the importance or meaning of this question, or even to identify the works associated with the term.

It is a question I take very seriously as a movie maker who also works as a theorist, because I have consciously chosen to make works that are actively engaged in their own theorization—not in an academic sense, but in a pragmatic, direct fashion—the question of "experimental" and "experimentation" has an urgency for me, as someone making movies, as a viewer watching the finished piece, and in relation to those few festivals specifically engaged with this type of motion picture work.

It is a question that has haunted my thinking since I first studied film and video production at a time when the two were generally considered as more-or-less incompatible in every way. And while it might be tempting to adopt the claim made that these works are "avant-garde"—that they are experiments in creating new kinds of experiences—this claim is also unsatisfying since both period styles and movements within the history of "experimental film" or "experimental video" area are well established. The avant-garde position is rhetorical, at best: the designation "experimental" has been a highly contested one by both artists and critics, who have all proposed various alternatives, equally unsatisfying. My solution has been to try and approach this issue semiotically.

Nevertheless, the "experimental" description has stuck with the greatest tenacity to this variety of media work.
Considered in relation to the dominant, mass media productions of commercial film and television, historically the "experimental" certainly appears to be a type of R&D for advertising. Yet, a definition on any of these terms transforms these works, created as artworks, into nothing more than unpaid innovations consumed by a market hungry for novelty, but unwilling to sponsor its creation. Neither is the scientifically rigorous, empirical "experiment" the way to understand "experimental cinema." Treating them as simply formal or scientific experiments eliminates the possibility of a resistant or subversive practice before it can even be considered. This definition is reductively formal and has no place for the critical and subjective meanings that are the main characteristic of this variety of media production.

The ways that 'experimental production' acts, as Edward Small noted in his book theorizing experimental media, as "a type of theory, a manifest, immediate, direct theory that bypasses the limiting intervention of separate semiotic systems, especially the spoken or written language upon which the accepted history of film theory depends"[1] that become apparent at the experimental festival, unlike the "experimental film" section at commercial festivals that more often function as catch-all's for work that doesn't fit elsewhere in their programs.

However, resolving the idea of 'experimental' does not answer the question, *"What is Experimental in 'Experimental Cinema'?"*—answering *this* question depends on the second part, this *"cinema."* The emergence of cinematic ideas, like any cultural phenomenon, begins with those communities whose shared experiences and common values enable an abstraction to exist. "Cinema" is such a shared cultural invention. The nature of viewership at the experimental festival enables an answer dependent on the 'experiment': the ability to theorize the nature of cinema from *within* motion pictures is unlike other theorizations precisely because of the demonstrative, immanent focus—these "experiments" are not reducible to a mechanical series of empirical relations, linear and circumscribed a priori.

This idea, "experimental cinema," is not necessarily coincident with the Modernist framework implied by Edward Small's "direct theory," which can suggest the "self-critical" purity of Clement Greenberg's painterly formalism. The reflexive engagement with the semiotic and formal codes that Small describes *may resemble* a Modernist formalism, or it *may not*, depending on what the work actually does: reductivism is the watchword for Greenberg's theory. This view is not the only way to comprehend experimental cinema. As an artist exploring these larger issues of "cinema," the experimental festival is essential to these theoretical concerns that lie beyond the individual motion picture. Relationships emerging in the theater between audience::screen, as well as the hidden order of programmed work that is shown, versus other works left unprogrammed— cultural/aesthetic hierarchies of taste built into this logic of selection and exclusion—make the experimental festival's role in the construction of "cinema" decisive in ways that both white cube and telescreen can never be.

While this construct is necessarily limited, this limitation is not cause for alarm—editorial choices are the reality of all programming decisions made under every circumstance: the concern is not with *bias* per se, but what the *results* of bias are—what/whose works are being discounted *a priori*, denied access, rejected? Experimental festivals tend towards an

why
(notes on the White Cube-Black Box-Telescreen Triad)

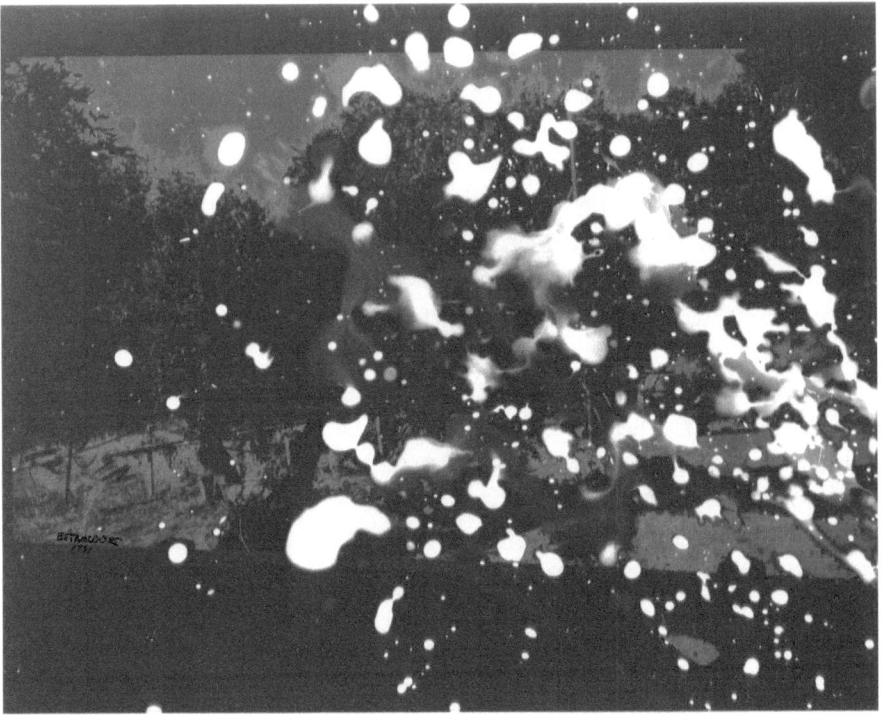

Exploding Photograph—unique process darkroom photograph, 1991

inclusive consideration that is broader and more accepting of variation than a commercial festival can be by nature. The different programmed 'shows' provide a way to engage with inevitable bias—bias becomes visible as/in the curation itself. This type of critical engagement within the experimental field produces a vibrant juxtaposition of works on two levels—within individual programs, and between the programs, making the experimental festival a specifically discursive event that always addresses the "cinematic."

Notions of what this *cinematic* is lie within all the historical (Modernist, Formal) attempts to define motion pictures, and serve as the unifying dimension in their organization as "important" to the history of motion pictures, the experimental festival is always a part of this process, while the white cube is not; that is the distinction between them. In the experimental festival, the unifying focus on "cinema" makes it possible for us to share the idea implied in the groupings themselves; for the white cube "art" substitutes for this focus, resulting in a radically different aesthetic and relationship to "cinema." The staged dialogue of different works—and implicitly between those works' makers—at festivals is particular to their construction of "cinema." Individual motion pictures gain nuance through their juxtaposition with other works—in context they have the opportunity to 'converse' through their medium.

What is of interest in screening at experimental festivals is not simply about audience or credentials or egotism: this event is where the concept "cinema" emerges. Only through the relationships between different works, eminent and remembered, does it become possible to distinguish and consider the idea of "cinema." This understanding is neither transcendent, nor materialist, but contextual. To participate in the festival as an artist has to do with this desire to engage the "cinematic" and all that it entails—the *reason* for wanting to show motion pictures in a film festival—otherwise, why bother?

The telescreen does not challenge this idea of the "cinematic" as much as alienate the idea of cinema. As digital technology became more powerful during the 1990s and Internet connection speeds rapidly increased, a third venue emerged for motion pictures—the computer monitor. As this screen has developed into portable ("touch") devices, it has come uncoupled from its former location and become instead a free floating, *un*sited screen quite distinct from the theater and gallery, fostering a type of viewing entirely different than what happens in those locations, posing the question of "*what is the cinematic*" once again, but in an entirely new sense. As Internet-based presentations of video have encouraged an integration of this medium into everyday life, these new engagements happen in a fashion that expands upon (is an outgrowth from) the ways that television historically became a mundane part of most households. This quotidian existence is what the telescreen has accentuated, bringing motion pictures anywhere the screen can go, and encouraging a third type of viewership that is distinct from the viewing relations common to so-called "white cube and black box" settings.

The telescreen is the contrary of the white cube/black box: the quotidian integration of life and art enabled by the telescreen is one where the 'considered' viewing common to both white cube (art gallery) and black box (theater) becomes 'distraction.' Questions of the supposed distance or proximity between the art world and experimental cinema[2] are irrelevant to this consideration. For this analysis, what is of interest is the *role* different types of presentation have for the movie maker in constructing the 'cinematic.'

Much has been written about the relationships artists and filmmakers have with the art world's white cube exhibition spaces. In contrast, very little has been said about the relationship between black box and telescreen: what appears in its place are discussions about the internet distribution of motion pictures instrumentally—as a broadcasting or publishing technology enabling a "democratic" distribution. That contemporary festivals rely upon these "digital screeners" submitted either formally or informally (via links shared in email) is notably missing in the analysis of relationships between white cube, black box and telescreen. This omission is especially interesting since it has become standard for curating and programming media works in both black box and white cube. While this shift is almost certainly as much an economic one as it is logistical, this practice brings the telescreen inherently into the presentation of works in sites utterly different from it.

What distinguishes these venues from the telescreen is precisely their situated-ness: they happen in a specific space and/for a specific duration. Unlike works seen on the telescreen, they are *events.* When the event occurs, it can take the form of spectacle (as is so often the case with commercial feature films), but this is not necessarily always the case—an event can be as simple as a private screening or exhibition for a close-knit community, or as public as a festival; an event is defined by the unifying nature of a shared experience in a particular place and time.

The collapse of distribution into exhibition is specific to the telescreen, a factor which renders it entirely different than (most) art gallery shows and all theatrical screenings: even when an event streams live to the theater, it still employs the conditions of theater—specific duration, curtain time, location—and not 'on demand' as with Internet-based distribution. The distinction between telescreen and black box is not simply a matter of distribution: technical differences of image scale, viewer engagement, and status of the work are determinant of these 'venues.' Unlike the motion picture shown in an art gallery that always already exists in an inherent relationship to painting where the audience is in transit *before* the image. The 'black box' screening follows the conventions of (live) theater with its "captive" audience seated and watching.

The telescreen accentuates a quotidian existence that emerged with television, emergent with a particular style of distracted viewing that often happens while doing something else. Differences in screen size and presentation style between these types of viewership reflect their different demands and the consequently different types of engagement accompanying each venue.

For an artist working with motion pictures, each of these situations poses radically different challenges both to form and structure of the work. While complex durational works are more easily apprehended by the majority of their audience in the

why
(notes on the White Cube-Black Box-Telescreen Triad)

theatrical setting, for most viewers in the art gallery these works become difficult to view—if only because the art gallery rarely includes the seating needed for such viewing. The various demands imposed by white cube and black box are well theorized and recognized; the telescreen's demands are not so familiar.

And these demands are not simply those posed by an unknown context, or the diminished size of the images, but the very conditions they're seen under: unlike the concerted gaze of the black box where the audience is literally captive, or the disinterested gaze of the white cube, the telescreen introduces a quotidian gaze. *Entertain me* is the ground state for this quotidian spectator—entertain me *en passant*—my attention will be held only until the next momentary distraction. The audience for ambient media is only partially engaged. Since it is simply one distraction among many, it only receives partial consideration. The telescreen fills a few minutes here, a pause, an accompaniment to something else. This relationship is entirely unlike the directed attention of both white cube and black box—however distinct they are from each other, they are still more alike than different when compared to the telescreen, and that is why this new third venue challenges the nature of the cinematic fundamentally.

While the formal devices of cinema have become commonplace throughout the art world, and the recombinative dimensions of montage have become a definitional feature and condition of contemporary cultural production, the nature of "cinema" as a distinct mode comes into question not because of its dominance, but because it seems poorly suited to the quotidian gaze common to the telescreen. This acknowledgement is not a criticism but a recognition of this change. This newly emergent mode demonstrates, not the insignificance of earlier venues, but their role in the construction of "cinema." The challenge to "cinema" posed by the telescreen is its fundamental rupture with the critical engagements with media implicit in the quotidian gaze. The distracted viewing common to the telescreen is not a type of watching capable of producing a critical understanding precisely because *criticism* requires attention to detail—the one thing that is missing from the quotidian gaze *by definition*. Black box presentations, of which the film festival is the most prominent, are specifically concerned with the type of engaged, critical viewing (and what the experimental film festival exists to promote) is what interests me as an artist looking to show my work to others: while the telescreen enables a wide distribution of work to *potentially* critical viewers in isolation, those viewers are specifically collected at the experimental festival in particular— the event draws them together—allowing for a robust audience particularly interested in critical consideration. Without these exhibitions, this historically-received idea of "cinema" becomes something no longer open to discussion, it begins to seem a "given"—which is how most commercial work approaches and accepts the idea 'cinema.' Only the experimental festival offers alternatives to what has been taken as a given, accepted without question.

About the Author

Michael Betancourt is an artist/historian, critical theorist, and curator. His essays have been translated into Chinese, French, Greek, Italian, Persian, Portuguese, and Spanish; journals such as *Leonardo, Semiotica* and *CTheory* have published his essays; he has edited five books on visual music technologies invented by artists such as Thomas Wilfred, Mary Hallock-Greenewalt, and Oskar Fischinger. In the course of this research, he discovered the oldest surviving hand-painted abstract films, done in 1916 by inventor and artist Mary Hallock-Greenewalt. He wrote about visual music's intersection with abstract film and motion graphics in his book *The History of Motion Graphics: From Avant-Garde to Industry*.

As an artist, he has exhibited his movies, site-specific installations, and non-traditional art forms in unseen, unusual, or public spaces since 1992. His movies work with the techniques of optical printing, but in a digital medium. His movies have been shown at in galleries, festivals and art fairs internationally. The second edition of his book, (written as a textbook), *Structuring Time* came out in 2009.

He is Professor of Motion Media Design at the Savannah College of Art and Design in Savannah, Georgia where he teaches the history of abstract film/video, visual music, motion graphics and video art. His work is archived at michaelbetancourt.com.

References

[1] Edward Small. *Direct Theory: Experimental Film/Video as a Major Genre* (Carbondale: Southern Illinois University Press, 1994), p. xv.
[2] Erika Balsom. "Brakhage's sour grapes, or notes on experimental cinema in the art world," MIRAJ 1.2

Dear Experiments in CinemaBook,
Notes From a Curmudgeon

By: Charles Lum

Of us involved over 50yo, actually acclimated in an age without the Internet (or cellphones!—OMG), Festivals were the only way. Which or wherever your clever inclinations would go: Gay, Underground, Sci-Fi, Sex... there were always a group of like-minded Freaks Gathering who you might even get to smell. And from that heady beginning, how could a You-Tube even compete? That's because it's really I-tube, as in Isolation. Unless it's streamed to one of those terrifyingly mesmerizing mega-mammoth new flat screen TVs, it's still a small screen, Individual Experience with only an imagined fellow audience: 6 Million hits... me too! OK I know your friends watch it too, but when? Not with you.

What fun is that?

Or worse yet is the watching on a tablet or way worser still, an I-Phone. What can you actually see on something that small? All I can think of when I see people staring into their smartphones (they rarely look away now) is unfortunately how I'd need one of those gigantic magnifying-lens-on-a-stand thingees that families used with their tiny TVs in the fifties. Now it's actually like some weird Fifties sci-fi itself with a zombie-fied populace, colliding chaotically into each other, following mysteriously transmitted orders from bright electronic tethers. And masses must be physically changing too, I mean how can they use those minuscule keyboards without their digits evolving into tiny tapered tappers? Inadvertent bumping is now the main form of public contact. Oops. Don't look at me. It's harder to walk in cities now, anywhere in the world. People don't pay attention to their surroundings.

Global Hypnosis!

As an old hippie, I'm much more attuned to the small group experience. I'm a swinger!

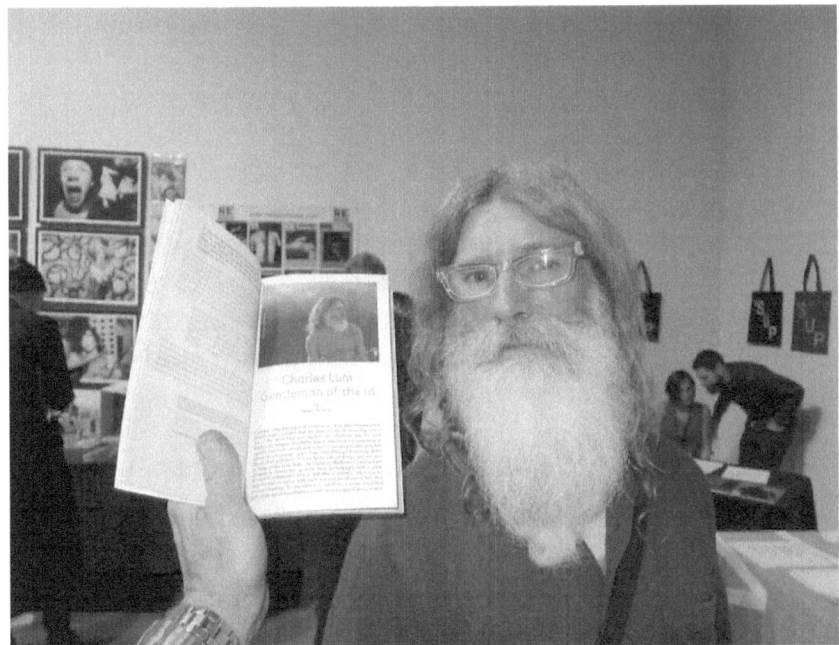

Self Portrait—Charles Lum

And festivals are like that… a swinger's party. You can physically meet the people who screen the films, the ones who made them, and the two, threes, and fours who watch them. You may or may not have met them before online or in face, and there may even be a meeting of someone who you would never have ever have dreamed of meeting before and…

What FUN is that!

Really kids, go outside and see the world, then come inside and feel it together.

To combat the ubiquity of filmed material available on demand and in hand, the film festivals I have long attended are no longer expanding cinematically, but by necessity, are expanding their physicality. From photos in the lobby, to festival parties, to art & concert performances, to commissioned plays, film festivals have grown or closed or merged to offer enough viable alternatives to entice audiences to experience ostensibly the same (sometimes free) stuff they get at home/on phone at will, in a communal public environment: a new type of Workshop & Show! This makes them even more inclusive for a wider art audience, but I worry that film festival attendance will forever be a problem in a world with ever expanding home theatre, (inflationary flat screens at deflationary prices) the proliferation of content, (Thank You! You-Tube and all it's spawn) and most importantly, the proliferation of those teeny tiny tablet platforms that the ever swelling merger and mammoth and mightier media corporations are ready to fill up with their own profitability as only agenda.

While there is now an infinite space and time continuum in which to broadcast our proto-cinematic-perhaps-once-filmed art, the intimacy and immediacy of a film festival in a warm space is increasingly precious in our busy electronic lives and even more important to us personal makers, in that for all the broadcast spectrum in the universe there is still a place to be seen in and as a real live and farting human.

Curmudgeonly yours,

Charles Lum
aka
clublum
November 24, 2014

About the Author

Charles Lum, aka clublum, received his MFA in Photography from the School of The Art Institute of Chicago in 2004 after 25 years scouting & managing locations for TV commercials and classic feature films like "Wall Street," "Fatal Attraction" & "Sid & Nancy." His short videos have screened globally in art and film venues.

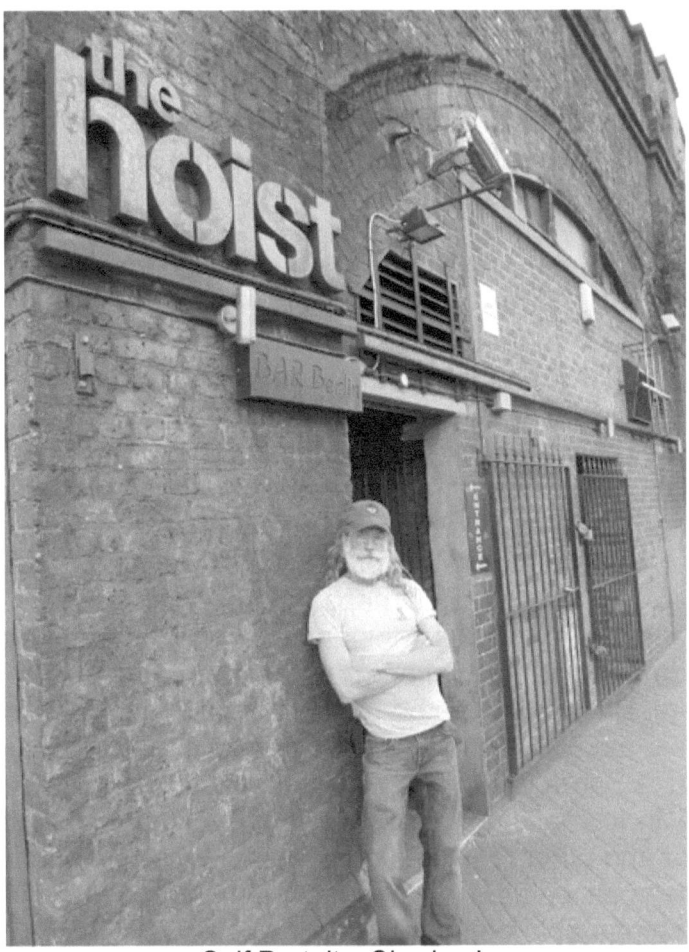

Self Portait—Charles Lum

What Makes "Experiments in Cinema" Such a Great Festival?

By: Caryn Cline

Experiments in Cinema in Albuquerque, NM is an ideal festival for experimental filmmakers: older and younger, working in film or digital, hugging the edges of more traditional storytelling structures or out there making media "like we've never seen it before," in the words of festival director Bryan Konefsky. As a filmmaker, I look forward to the deep conviviality and generosity of spirit that the festival exudes. What makes this festival so terrific? Here are some of the ingredients that strike me as crucial:

An inherent feminism. This may seem an odd ingredient to begin with, but it is true of EIC and it is important. In league with the Independent Imaging Retreat in Ontario (founded by Marian McMahon and Phil Hoffman), EIC is one of the few not overtly women-centered filmmaking organizations or festivals that is downright enthusiastic about the contributions women make repeatedly to the medium, every year. About half of the films shown each year are by women directors or have significant contributions by women in major positions, and not just as producers. The other, and perhaps far more significant achievement, is that EIC is constantly training smart, talented young women to be festival programmers, producers, and filmmakers. Bryan may be the public face of this organization, but working alongside him are Michelle Mellor and Beth Hansen and Sahra Saedi and Jenette Isaacson and many others. Without making a big deal out of it, EIC is walking the walk that I and other feminists of my generation (the second wave) imagined we'd be walking much earlier in our lives— creating comparable opportunities for women in this most male dominated of fields.

Hospitality and Conversation. EIC understands that one of the big draws of a film festival for filmmakers is the opportunity to meet other filmmakers and programmers, to talk about our work together. Most festivals I've been to recently either forego hospitality altogether (they can't afford it or can't find people to manage it or don't think it is important), or they host "after parties" where the music is so loud that there is no possibility of talking to anyone without seriously damaging your vocal cords. Every night at EIC there is something to do after the screenings—a chance to get together and talk over food and beverages at one of the venues that supports the festival. There's often music, but it isn't so loud that you can't talk to one another. In addition, Bryan and his partner Patti host a potluck brunch every year for filmmakers and friends of the festival. After each screening, there is a conversation among the makers in that "experiment" [a one hour group of films] and the audience.

Deep organizational support. EIC does such a good job in part because it has three other organizations (at least) that support it in various ways. One is Basement Films, the non-profit under whose umbrella EIC is produced. Basement Films houses a jaw-dropping archive of found footage films and runs workshops all year. It also has memberships, and these two outreach strategies help build an audience for experimental work in the community. The second organization is the Guild Theater, an old movie house in the Nob Hill neighborhood run by Keif Henley, a man whose deep love of cinema and knowledge about projection allow EIC to screen work in 35mm, 16mm, and digitally. The work always looks and sounds superb. Keif is also a founder of Basement Films. The third organization is the University of New Mexico, Department of Cinematic Arts, where faculty member Nina Fonoroff, is herself an experimental filmmaker. Bryan is on the faculty there, and the University provides both umbrella support for grants, as well as space for workshops. In addition, Bryan offers a class on film festival producing. His students get credit for—get this—

actually helping produce the festival. In addition, each "experiment" (program) opens with an "interstitial" piece created by a small team of student filmmakers. Each piece incorporates and introduces the films in the upcoming "experiment." So, students in the class gain experience as both producers and makers. I hope they know how lucky they are to have such opportunities.

A Variety of Workshops. Each year, EIC offers a series of workshops for filmmakers and interested audience members. These workshops are free to festival goers. (I've been fortunate enough to be able to present a workshop there for several years in a row.) The offerings are eclectic and they evolve. There have been workshops in film hand-processing, animation, acting, camera operating, non-camera filmmaking, found footage filmmaking, and many other topics of interest to filmmakers looking to juice their practice and to filmgoers who want to make the leap to filmmaking. Hopefully, one day soon Keif Henley will teach a workshop in 16mm projector repair and maintenance.

International Reach. EIC has a brilliant strategy for getting the work and the word out. Every year, the organization produces a series of DVDs with the work from that festival on it. As a filmmaker, you are asked whether it is OK for EIC to include your film in their collection. (Say yes.) The festival collection is programmed at other festivals and venues around the world, in Serbia, Germany, South Korea, Peru, Argentina, and many other places. As a filmmaker associated with EIC, your films will travel. As experimental filmmakers, we know that we are not in it for the money. Ours is a "no commercial value" artistic practice, fortunately. For a very small investment on our part (the festival submission fee—which is waived once you've had something screened at the festival), our films can travel, even if we can't afford to. At the same time, EIC brings collections of films (and filmmakers) to Albuquerque each year. I've seen bodies of work from Serbia, Italy, China, Spain, South Korea,

France, and Germany as part of the festival. One memorable live performance piece featured a French media artist who had recently performed in North Korea. At EIC in Albuquerque, one feels the global reach of experimental filmmaking practices.

Obviously, film festivals and venues arise in all kinds of ways, with all kinds of support, or no support. There is no one "right way" or "template" that works for every festival in every community. But EIC sets a standard to be understood, appreciated, celebrated and perhaps even emulated. Were I to try to start a film festival, I would study their model closely. As it approaches its 10th anniversary, I wish Experiments in Cinema 10 more years and then 10 more after that.

About the Author

Caryn Cline is a filmmaker and teacher who lives and works in Seattle, Washington. Her short experimental, animated, and "botanicollage" films have appeared in national and international festivals. Besides making films, she teaches people how to create handmade botanicollage films.

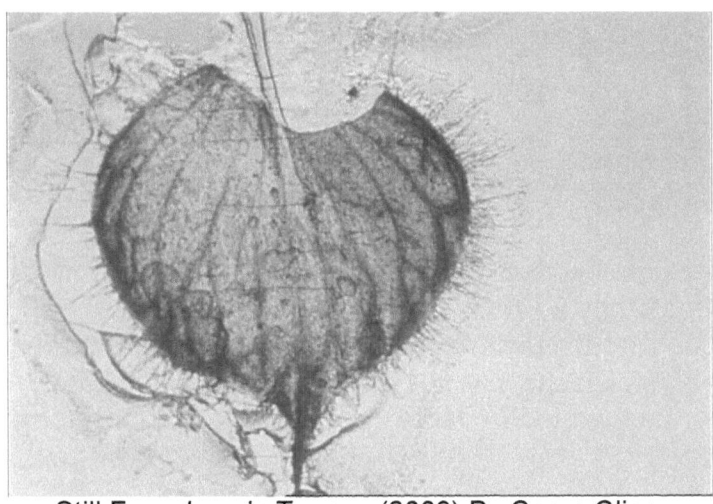

Still From *Lucy's Terrace* (2009) By Caryn Cline

Alexie Dmitriev

I Fell in Love with a French Man

By: Alexie Dmitriev

Once upon a time when I was 19, I saw a film titled *Dies Irae* at a festival that doesn't exist anymore. It was the second experimental film I ever saw in my life (the first being *Papillon d'amour* by Nicolas Provost). I'd already made my first found footage film a couple of months before, but this piece just opened my eyes on what amazing things can be done in this genre. That summer (or spring, I can't recall), I swore to hunt down the director of this film and befriend him or her.

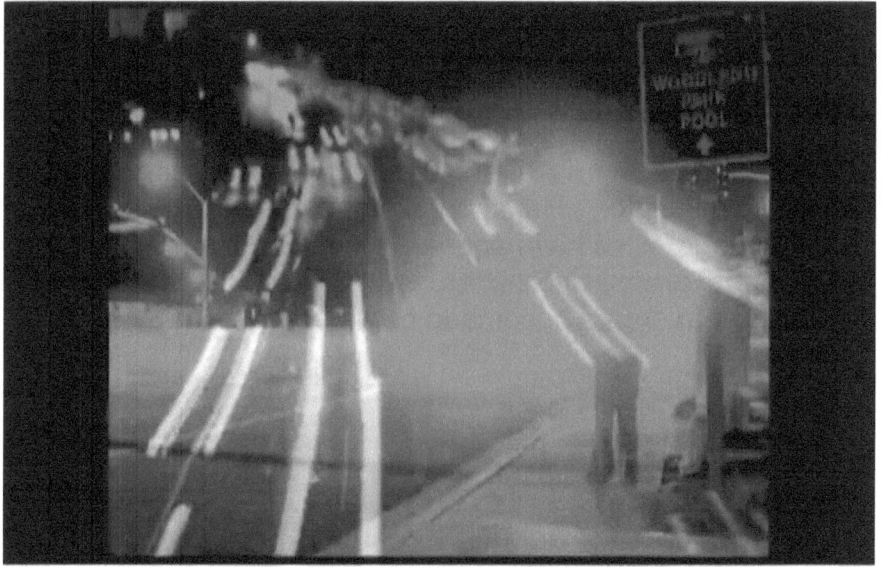

Still from *Dies Irae* (2005) By Jean-Gabriel Périot

With the cunning use of the Internet, I discovered that the film was directed by a French man named Jean-Gabriel Périot. After googling his pictures and interviews, I found more of his earlier films, which were not as good as the one I saw in the cinema. So I wrote the name down and waited for our next encounter.

Over the next three to four years, Jean-Gabriel produced two more masterpieces, and I started a company (which organized his first retrospective in Russia) and didn't have time to make any films until 2009. Then I quit my job and decided to walk the Earth.

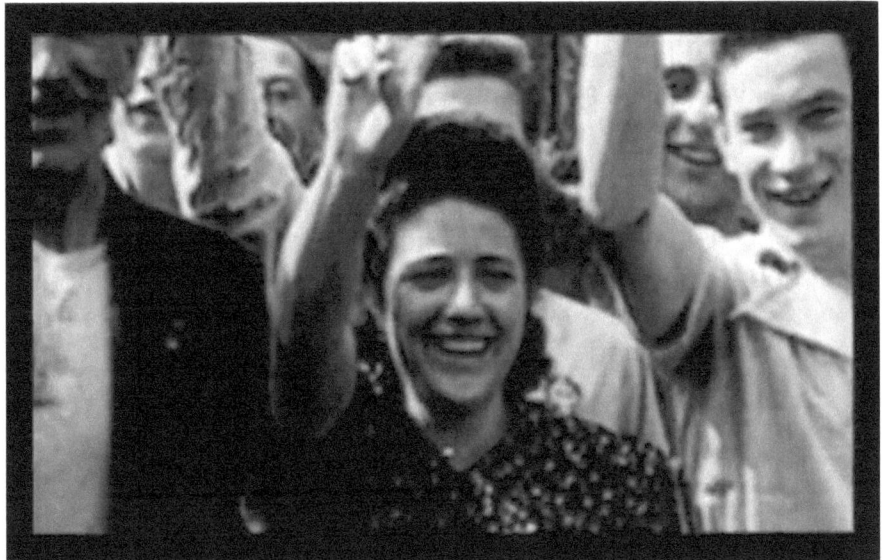

Still from *Even if She had Been a Criminal* (2006) By Jean-Gabriel Périot

In 2010, my walking the Earth took me to France. So I mailed Jean-Gabriel (as we already exchanged work correspondence) to ask him if he was up for meeting me. He told me that he was, but I had to be in the city of Tours by August 4th as he was moving to Paris the next day.

I arrived early in the morning a day before, and was killing time by roaming the city until the meeting. It turned out that I was in that very city 10 years ago. It also turned out that a third of the population are Japanese students. I bought a belt (still use it) and a small iron (it broke down the same year). Then the evening came and it was time to meet Jean-Gabriel.

He came to the bar with a bicycle and a friend wearing a purple shirt, green pants and some other brightly coloured garments (well, he looked like a rainbow). He asked me if I liked beer. I do like beer. He went into the bar and brought a carafe of 3 or 5 litres (convert it to American measurements yourself). I had never seen a French man that loved beer so much. He smoked his transparent roll-ups (I still had no clue how to roll) and had the same problem as I did—not looking into strangers' eyes while talking. It was awesome. He invited me to have coffee at his house the next day.

In the morning, I went over to his house on its last day of habitation. There was a mirror with a golden frame. One wall was green, another white. And there was a garden. Tomatoes, flowers, and whatnot. I was still tipsy. Early Placebo was playing while we had way too much coffee. I took my first picture of him. And then it was time to part.

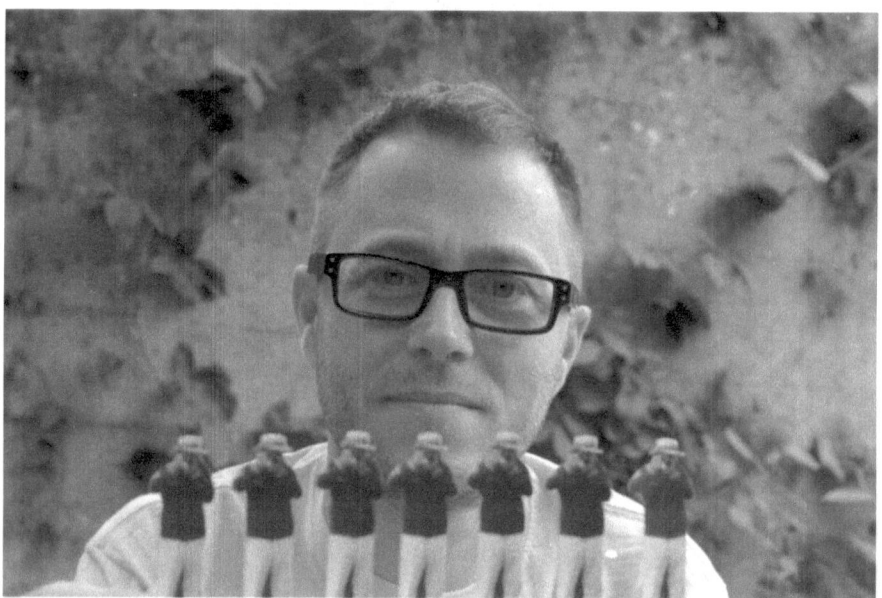

Portrait of Jean-Gabriel Périot by Alexie Dmitriev

Since then, Gabi (yes, I can call him that now) became my friend and my favourite filmmaker of all time. Since then, we've been together in Romania, Italy, France, etc. He even met my parents.

The last time we saw each other was in 2013 in New York. I was around for the Tribeca Film Festival (someone selected my film by mistake (link: https://vimeo.com/36266785) and he was coming back from a North American film tour. We had only one night before his flight back home, and as proper friends we decided to meet and hit the town.

It was in a surprisingly cool punk/rock bar with a smoking garden(!!!) in Brooklyn. Being Russian, I tend to buy drinks, but Gabi decided to get the first round (I think he had just gotten paid in Canada). It was loud and he has a French accent. So, I was enjoying a silent scene of him trying to understand what tap beer they had. As the bartender was getting angry because he couldn't get a word of what Gabi was saying, I stepped in and got us some drinks. Then it was smoking and talking. The bar started to close and before leaving we asked a random woman to take a picture of us. And her friend photobombed us.

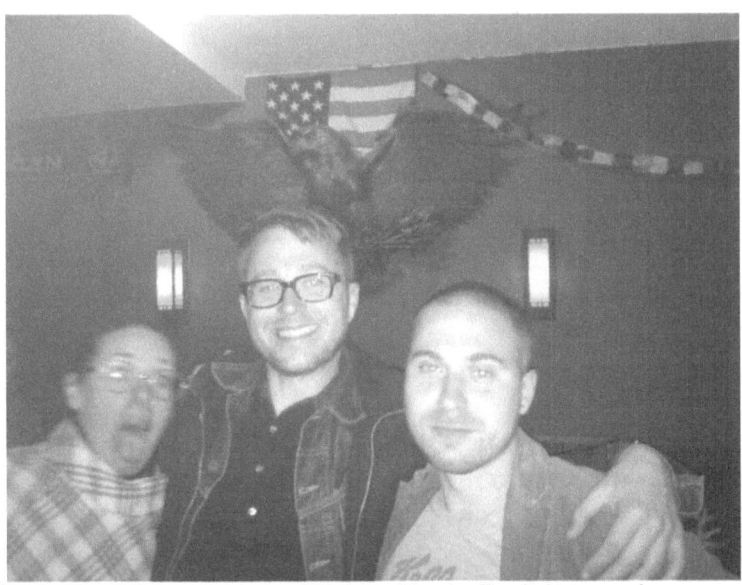

Portrait of Jean-Gabriel Périot, Alexie Dmitriev, and woman

We went outside and were strolling back to where he was staying when we saw a bar covered in tacky neon lights. It looked empty, so we decided to have our last shot there. We walked in: a huge bouncer and three tiny Latina ladies. It was a Puerto Rican bar, so Gabi decided to order in Spanish. Another scene, which ended with a barmaid telling him "You speak nothing." I got us two tequilas, then something else. We asked if they had karaoke. They didn't, but they thought that we were a couple and offered us to dance to Ricky Martin. We did. I don't remember the rest of the night—I woke up on a D-train with a piece of paper in my hand that was an invitation to a birthday party of one of the ladies at the bar. I texted Gabi to check if he caught his flight; he was already in the airport and it was morning. That was a good night.

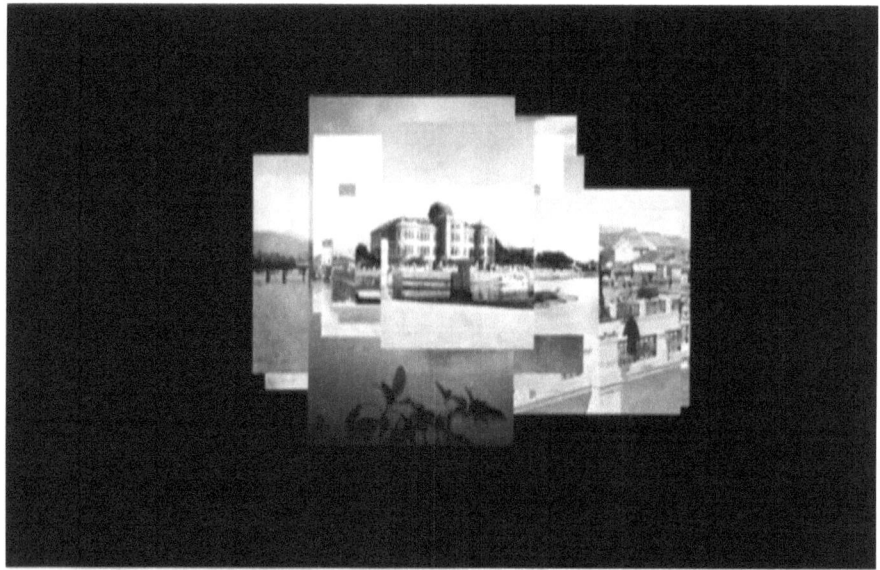

Still from *200000 Phantoms* (2007) By Jean-Gabriel Périot

Now he is finishing his first feature about German political terrorists, he dreams to move to Japan, and works way too much. I'm still lazy and produce an ultra-short film once every two years. I will see him a couple of times in 2015. We will drink more beer and maybe I will drag him into a karaoke bar. If you see this man—give him a hug and say hi. I miss him terribly.

About the Artist
"Since I was a little girl my dream was to star in an experimental film." – Alexie Dmitriev

---

Regional Support Network (RSN)

By: Clint Enns and Leslie Supnet

RSN is a nomadic screening series started in Toronto, Ontario out of a desire to show experimental moving images from other cities unmediated by a Toronto curatorial lens.[i] Explicitly, the work is not curated by RSN as we invite curators from other areas to present work from their community. The only condition is that the curator must be an active member of their community and that they must present their own work in the program. Through RSN, we are attempting to challenge a culture of moving image curation in Toronto, a place that we feel is in need of a paradigm shift away from old routines. The oppressive conservatism we struggle with politically in our day-to-day lives, we see in our community of experimental moving images and must be challenged with at least another voice to speak alongside the dominant ways of working. In addition, we are hoping to challenge Toronto moving-image aesthetics by allowing work to show that may offend our sensibilities, both in terms of content and form. What we desire is evolution.

By regionalism, RSN is simply referring to work made in different geographic regions or communities. With that in mind, we argue for a critical and fluid form of relational regionalism and argue that there are often distinctive local characteristics to be found in the work from one region since the work is implicitly informed by the artists' perception of and identification with their sense of place. Of course, we are not implying an aesthetic consistency to the work, however, we do believe that one's own community, dialogues within the community and physical landscape inevitably, at the very least subconsciously, inform one's artistic practice.

Amber Christensen, programmer of UNSCENE: Film and Video from Saskatchewan,[ii] poses the following concern in her programming statement:

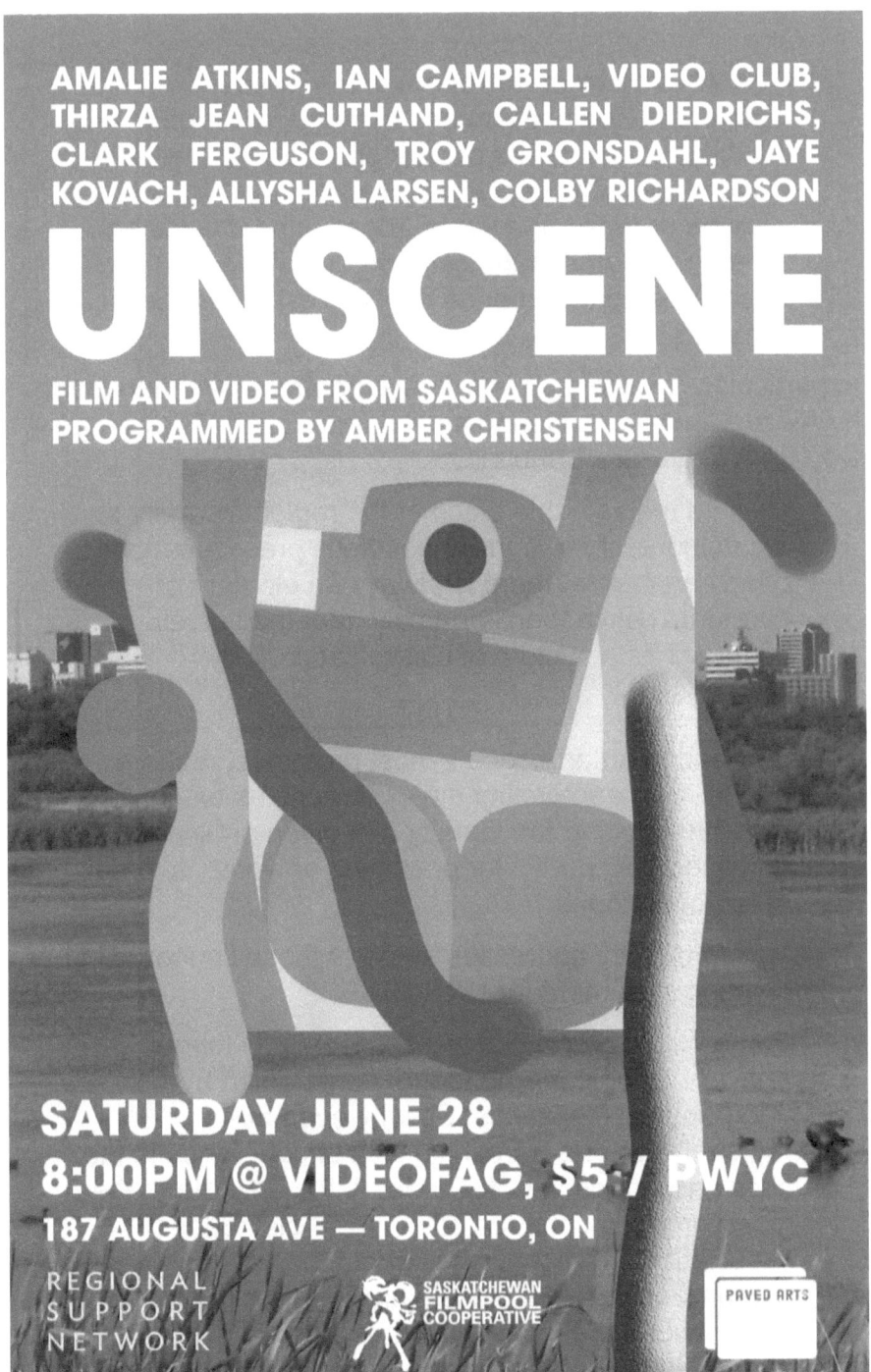

So what do we make of regionally based curatorial projects? Regionalism has become, somewhat, of a dirty word in terms of curatorial agendas with an understandable concern that surveys of regional art will be reduced to a set of tropes (wheat fields and decaying barns in the case of Saskatchewan), or a scene being determined by the most prominent makers.[iii]

In particular, Christensen is referencing an observation made by Alison Cooley in a Canadian Art article titled "They Made A Day Be A Day Here." She states,

Despite the valuable place of the regional survey as a catalogue of the current aesthetic preoccupations of any art centre, there is always an element of curatorial risk in them—namely, that the survey might act as a system of classification, only

delineating an art scene's most prominent makers, and then characterizing their practices as exemplary, thereby reducing the identity of a given art scene down to a few particular practices, or worse, to a set of regional tropes.[iv]

Christensen directly addresses some of these concerns in her programming statement for UNSCENE:

Some would argue that regionalism is no longer relevant, people are no longer constrained by geographical limitations. So why even talk regionalism? The refreshing lack of coherence in the films and videos in UNSCENE, is the antidote to the glossy images constructed by provincial tourism associations; regionalism is about the varying personal voices of a place along with the push and pull between the local and the rest of world. It's hard to deny that when you inhabit a particular place that

it doesn't seep into your work.[v]

In other words, Christensen acknowledges the role of space in influencing artistic production, in addition to commenting on the lack of aesthetic consistency.
RSN further attempts to reduce some of the risks involved in programming regional work by allowing artists to curate from their own communities, in essence, eliminating programs of simply the regions' most prominent artists. We are also quick to acknowledge that these types of programs are simply a survey of the work being produced in a particular region and may not necessarily be the best representatives of that region. That is, these programs aren't intended to be a greatest hits compilation, they are intended to present a cross-section of the work currently being produced from the perspective of artists that are engaging with their community.

If you are an engaged member of your experimental film community and you are interested in showing work from your region, feel free to contact us and we will do our best to set-up a screening with you in Toronto.

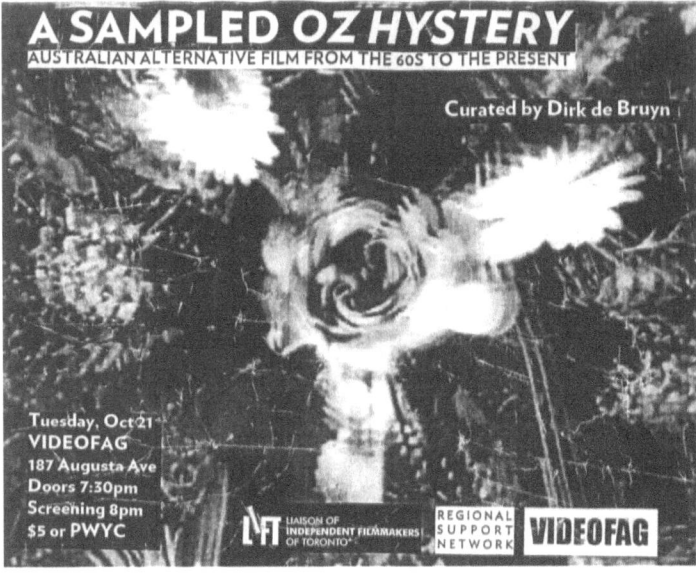

About the Artists

Clint Enns is a video artist and filmmaker living in Toronto, Ontario. His work primarily deals with moving images created with broken and/or outdated technologies. His work has shown both nationally and internationally at festivals, alternative spaces and microcinemas.

He has a Master's degree in mathematics from the University of Manitoba, and has recently received a Master's degree in cinema and media from York University where he is currently pursuing a PhD. His writings and interviews have appeared in Millennium Film Journal, Incite! Journal of Experimental Media and Spectacular Optical.

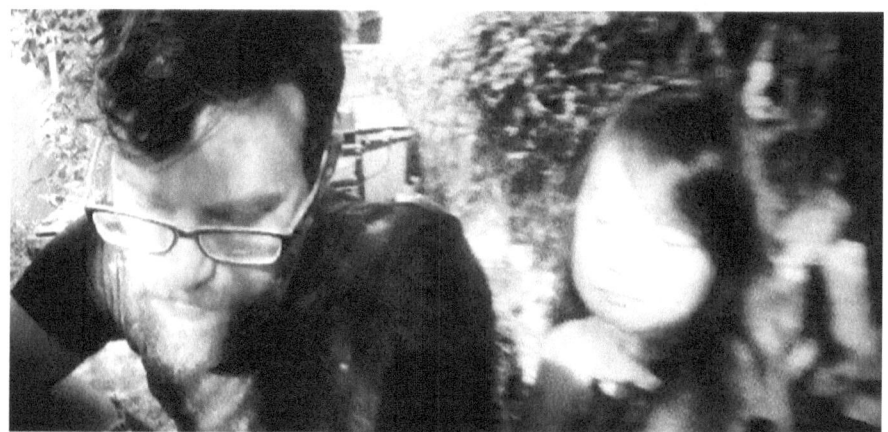

Portrait—Clint Enns and Leslie Supnet

Leslie Supnet is a Toronto-based moving image artist, originally from Winnipeg, MB. Supnet utilizes animation, found images + sound, lo-fi and experimental practices to create documents of her personal vision. She is currently pursuing her MFA at York University, and teaches animation workshops with various artist-run centres.

Her work has screened at microcinemas, galleries and film festivals such as Oberhausen International Short Film Festival,

Toronto International Film Festival, Images Festival, Antimatter, Melbourne International Animation Festival and various others. She has curated short programs for the Winnipeg Cinematheque, and co-curated programs for DIM Cinema, Plastic Paper and Regional Support Network.

References

[i] The idea for series was the result of a conversation with scholar and curator Eli Horwatt. We would like to thank all of the many people who have helped make these screenings possible, in particular, all of the moving image artists, curators and projectionists who have worked with RSN, VideoFag, Analog Preservation Network, LIFT, PAVED Arts, Saskatchewan Filmpool Cooperative and Images Festival.

[ii] UNSCENE was presented by Regional Support Network in collaboration with VideoFag, PAVED Arts and Saskatchewan Filmpool Cooporative on June 28, 2014 at VideoFag in Toronto, Ontario.

[iii] Amber Christensen, "UNSCENE: Films and Videos From Saskatchewan Programmed by Amber Christensen." Available here: http://amberdchristensen.tumblr.com/post/92166004881/curated-program-film-and-video-from-saskachewan (accessed October 29, 2014).

[iv] Alison Cooley, "They Made a Day Be Day Here: Prairie Positive," *Canadian Art* (January 16, 2013) http://www.canadianart.ca/reviews/2014/01/16/they-made-a-day-be-a-day-here/#sthash.NYJhkwYx.dpuf (accessed October 29, 2014).

[v] Christensen, "UNSCENE."

Come into the Fashion Zone

By: Chip Lord

In 1991, I lived in Tokyo for six months on a U.S. - Japan Friendship Fellowship. At the time, Japan had a booming economy and the bubble had not yet burst. U.S. companies were sending their executives over to study the "Japanese way." I lived in a neighborhood two stops outside the Metro loop and my transfer station was Ikebukuro. Above the subway station was a Seibu Department store. In early 1991 they mounted an ad campaign, "The Fashion Zone," to announce that fashion had come to Ikebukuro, an apparently bland neighborhood. The ad featured a western model, probably European, but possibly American and she was wearing a chic business suit. There was a TV spot which showed her strolling into an architectural manquque of the public space in front of the Seibu store, and she stood about nine stories tall in relation to the façade of Seibu. I thought that Godzilla must be the primary reference, though her walk was definitely from the runway. On the actual facade of Seibu was posted a close up shot of her face, about 50 feet tall, so that she stared out at passersby, an haute couture version of Big Brother. The

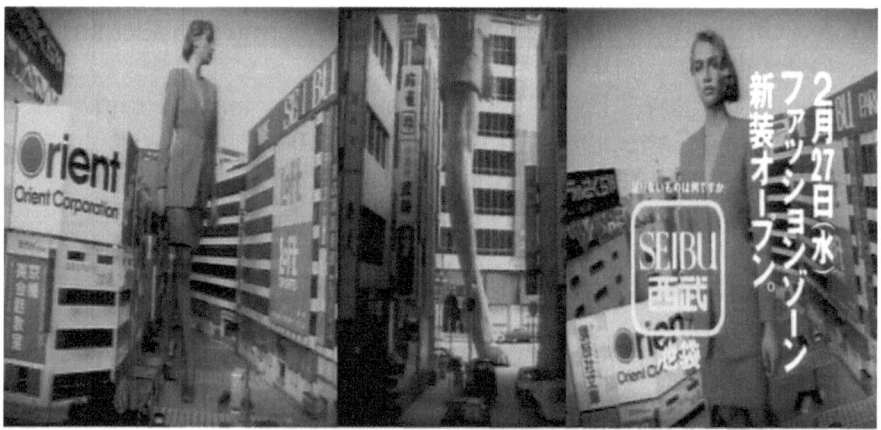

Stills from the Seibu TV Ad

campaign continued in the subway below Seibu, where a poster version showed a video still image. No one could miss this Fashion Zone statement.

I had a friend in Tokyo who was able to arrange a meeting with the creative director of the Ad agency that had produced this campaign. It turned out to be a "lost in translation" meeting. He didn't understand why I was interested to see the architectural model, and besides it was in storage and not available. And he couldn't answer my questions, "What was the creative source of this image and why was a western model chosen as the face of fashion in Ikebukuro?"

All of this is backstory for my installation, "FASHION ZONE." When I returned to the US, I built my own version of the architectural model, as an interactive video installation that viewers could enter and experience themselves the size of Godzilla. It had two live video cameras and a video loop shot in and around the Seibu Department store. This piece was shown at the Rena Bransten Gallery, San Francisco in 1992 and also at the New Museum, New York later that same year.

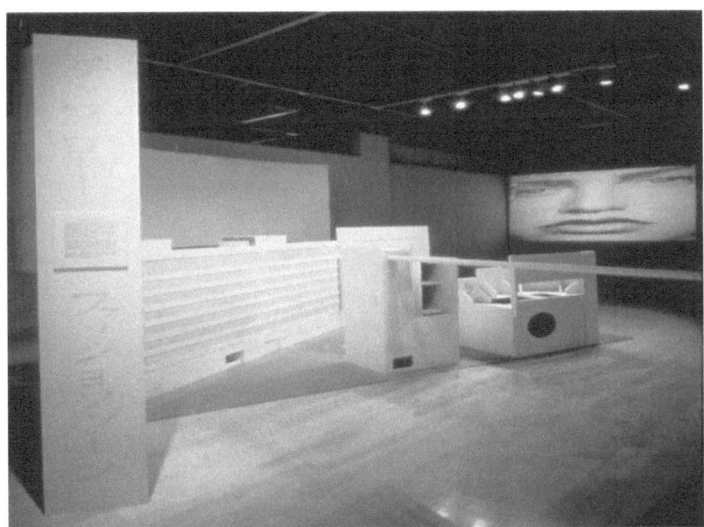

Fashion Zone installed at The Rena Bransten Gallery, San Francisco, 1993

About the Artist

Chip Lord is an artist who works with video and photography. His films, which straddle experimental and documentary approach, have been exhibited widely in festivals and museums. He is a Professor Emeritus in the Department of Film & Digital Media at UC Santa Cruz and he lives in San Francisco.

A Brief Look Back

By: Ben Popp

The first small cinema gathering I attended was in Milwaukee, Wisconsin, at the Riverwest Film Co-op back when it was located on Locust Ave. The event was a potluck, which happened once a month, called "Soup and Cinema." Folks showed up with all sorts of food before getting down to the business of devouring the works of film and video, which were brought to be screened. I was hooked right away by this little conclave of cinephiles and went to as many as I could during my short time living in that great city. It was enthralling to see works made by other people who were both in and out of the academic system. In this warm and welcoming studio, everyone was just a peer!

Upon moving back to Albuquerque to finish up a degree in the Media Arts program at the University of New Mexico, I sought out a similar close-knit community to the one I had seen in Milwaukee. I remember wandering into the now defunct Alphaville Video, and striking up a short conversation with Keif Henley about the organization Basement Films, which he was running at that time. I asked if I could put together an open screening and make it a Basement Films event. "Of course!" Keif said. Shortly thereafter, at Winnings Coffee shop, the first installation of Cinemus Publicus was born, supported largely by the folks of Basement Films and an energetic guy named Bryan Konefsky. The small community brought in films and videos of varying formats and lengths. We had a pretty great setup, if I remember right, where we could easily switch back and forth between film and video projections, and even toss in some live audio performances with the works. Not only were local filmmakers' works shown, but we sometimes screened works by well known filmmakers; Bruce Connor's "Mongoloid" by DEVO being a favorite memory of mine. In addition, folks from across the country in places like Chicago and Milwaukee sent

55

in work to screen for these film-loving Burqueños. For each event, I handcrafted posters to put up around town hoping we could bring the punk DIY aesthetic in the form of film and video to the community. An open door policy in which if you tried something out, you could come and show it!

During this time, Basement Films was also playing host to traveling film shows such as the Gaddabout's curated programs or the Tom Comerford and Bill Daniels touring show. I remember Tom and Bill's programs so well because when I moved to Chicago to get a masters degree at the School of the Art Institute of Chicago, where Tom taught, it was fun to come up to him and say "Hey, I saw your show in Albuquerque." To me, having seen these shows already began to break down some sort of barrier between established filmmakers and myself, for despite still being a student, on a peer level, we were part of the same small world of experimental filmmaking. This was very important and exciting, because unlike the rest of the art world in which one could only gain acceptance with their peers, at least in my opinion, one had to be a success as well. However, with this medium being so small, playful, and unique, if you showed up or participated, you were part of the club already!!

During the summer of 2007, I was able to go on a short film tour with my friend and co-filmmaker Kenny Reed, upon finishing our grad program in Chicago. I do not think I would have attempted this excursion had I not witnessed similar tours back in Albuquerque. I guess I always assumed you would have to be in a band to go on tour. It was a joy to be able to take that adventure as filmmakers. Along the way we met good friends and fellow makers who are still a part of our lives!

Later that year, I moved to Portland, Oregon, excited about the community because of everything I had heard. However the "scene" was at a crossroads when I landed, as if slowly being sucked back into the muddy banks of the Willamette River. The

PDX fest was only a couple years away from ending, and the institution I had hoped to be an all-inclusive film co-op such as

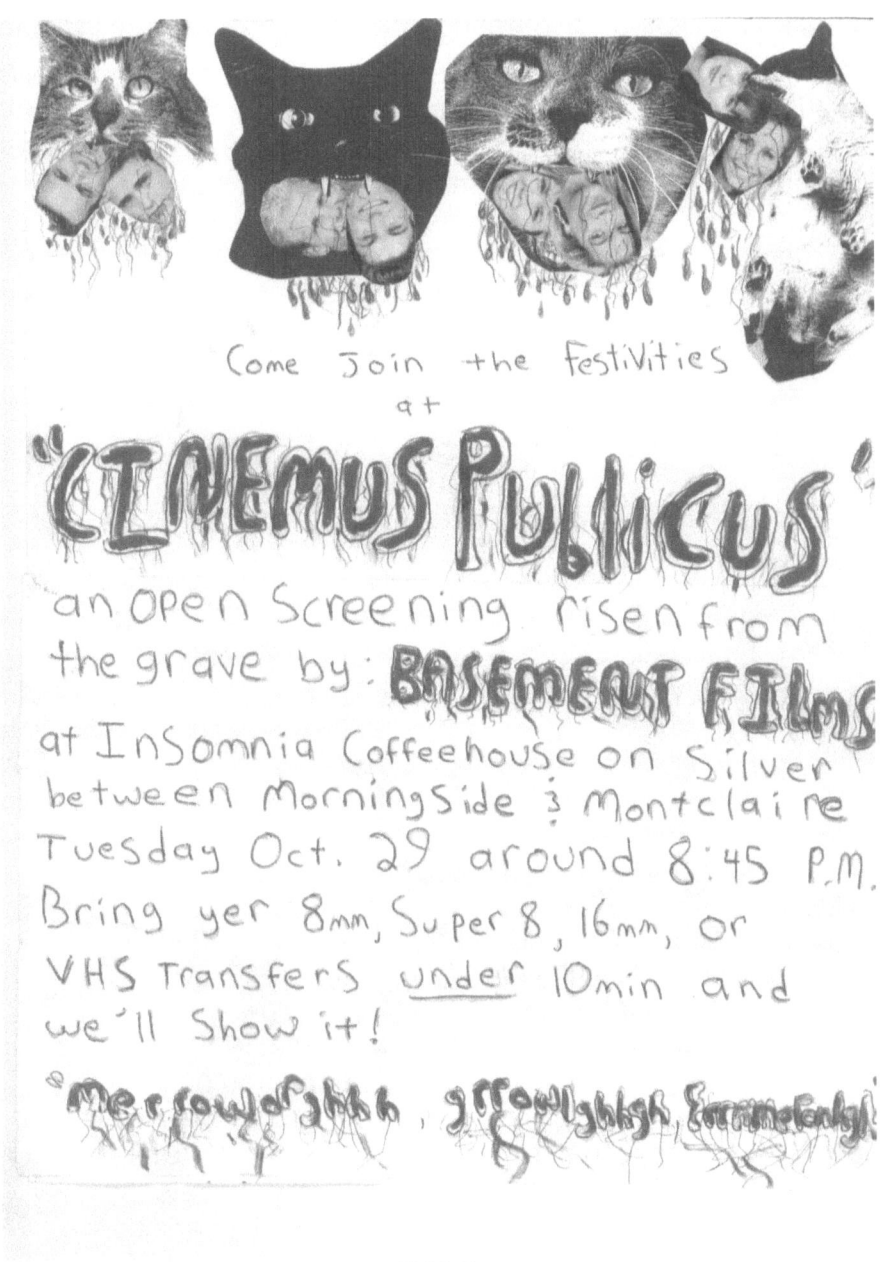

Come join the festivities at

"CINEMUS PUBLICUS"

an open screening risen from the grave by: BASEMENT FILMS

at Insomnia Coffeehouse on Silver between Morningside & Montclaire Tuesday Oct. 29 around 8:45 P.M. Bring yer 8mm, Super 8, 16mm, or VHS transfers <u>under</u> 10min and we'll show it!

(2002)

the Riverwest Co-op was a much larger institution with stricter rules of programming. I discovered the wonderful organization Cinema Project, but while they program amazing current and older works, the door for the local, traveling, or off the beat makers was not present. In the past, I was able to hitch myself to an already formed organization and go from there. I found that without this set cornerstone I was helpless, an unfortunate disposition I have, but what can you do?!

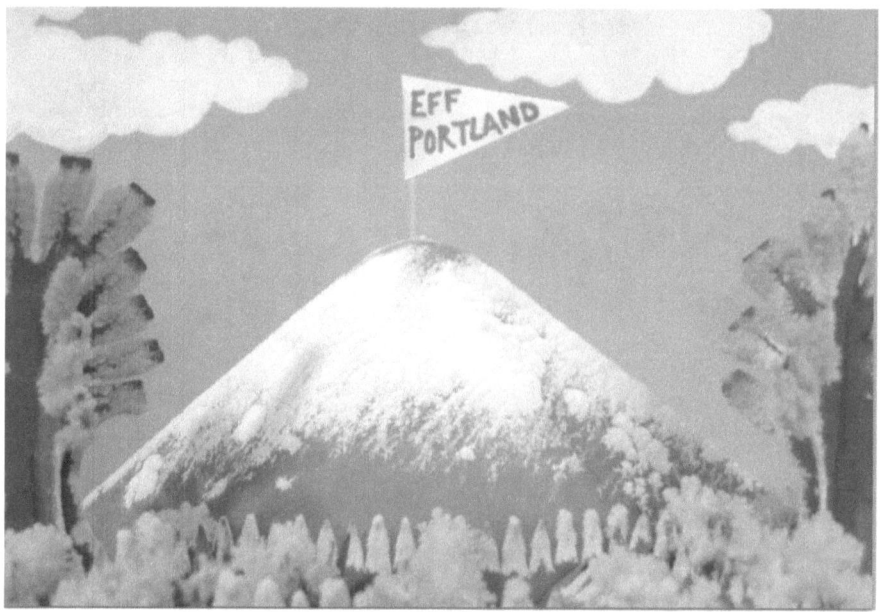

Luckily for me, I was determined to try and show my own work. After renting a projector for an event I had put together, I ran into a guy named Dustin Zemel. We hit it off while helping to explain the concept of installation to the fellow whom I had rented the projector from. Dustin and I met often afterwards and I can only imagine that I continuously peppered him with my desire of a space in which we could host screenings on the level I had witnessed across the country. In 2010, Dustin rented a studio, not just for his own work, but to help create this new screening space we had always talked about. In addition to myself, he brought to the table two other individuals, Karl Lind

and Hannah Piper Burns, whom I had not yet met. Together, we formed the organization Grand Detour. Starting in May of 2010 we began hosting screenings and talks not just for local filmmakers, but for artists using installation and sound works. Word got out that Portland suddenly had a hub once again, and we began to play host to those traveling through town on tours. Previously, when someone was in Seattle and going to San Francisco they simply skipped over Portland. No more.
We provided a net not just for those people, but also for those in town who, other than the Internet, had no other audience or place to screen their films!

After several seasons of continuous programming, there were shifts in personnel and we left the old studio of 2020.
We moved around to several different galleries, theaters, and music venues, all the while continuing to play host to a large array of amazing media makers from near and far. During this time, we also came to the realization that the heartbeat of the Portland experimental film scene, the PDX fest, was not going to return, or had been told that. We decided to pick up the ball and run. In Fall of 2011, Grand Detour formed the Experimental Film Festival Portland, and in May of 2012, with a Polaroid camera, Super 8 film, a homemade volcano, and way too many donuts, EFFPortland blasted onto the scene. During these past 3 years, EFFPortland has brought hundreds of incredible films, installations, and performances to Portland, emphasizing the community spirit I had first seen back at the Soup and Cinema and Cinemus Publicus. We also based our fest around the Experiments in Cinema fest, by which there are no awards, rather everyone is a winner for making killer films, and keeping the entry fees low to encourage folks to submit work.

Throughout all of this, we continued to host screenings for touring and local programmers and filmmakers on the micro side of things. To engage even more with the local community we also founded our own open screening/potluck called the Portland Stew, which has garnered a fun little community all

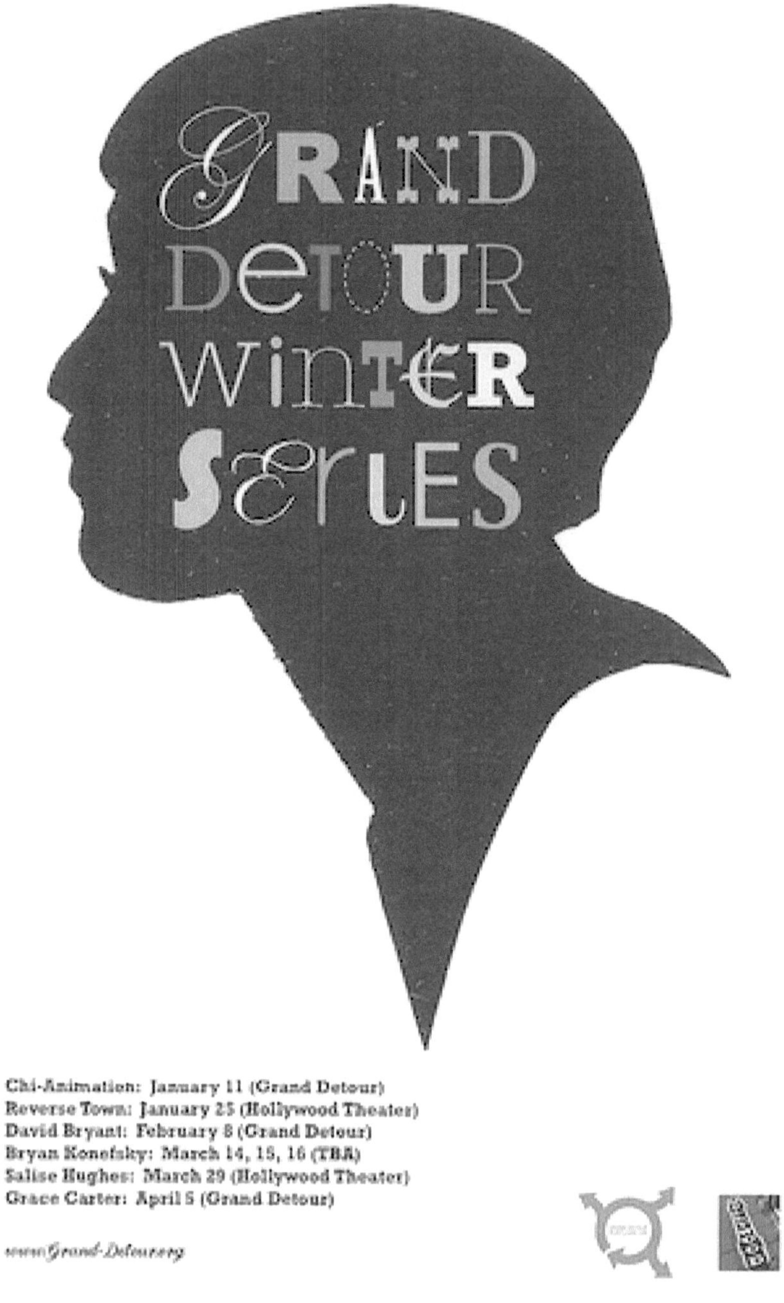

GRAND DETOUR WINTER SERIES

Chi-Animation: January 11 (Grand Detour)
Reverse Town: January 25 (Hollywood Theater)
David Bryant: February 8 (Grand Detour)
Bryan Konefsky: March 14, 15, 16 (TBA)
Salise Hughes: March 29 (Hollywood Theater)
Grace Carter: April 5 (Grand Detour)

www.Grand-Detour.org

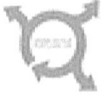

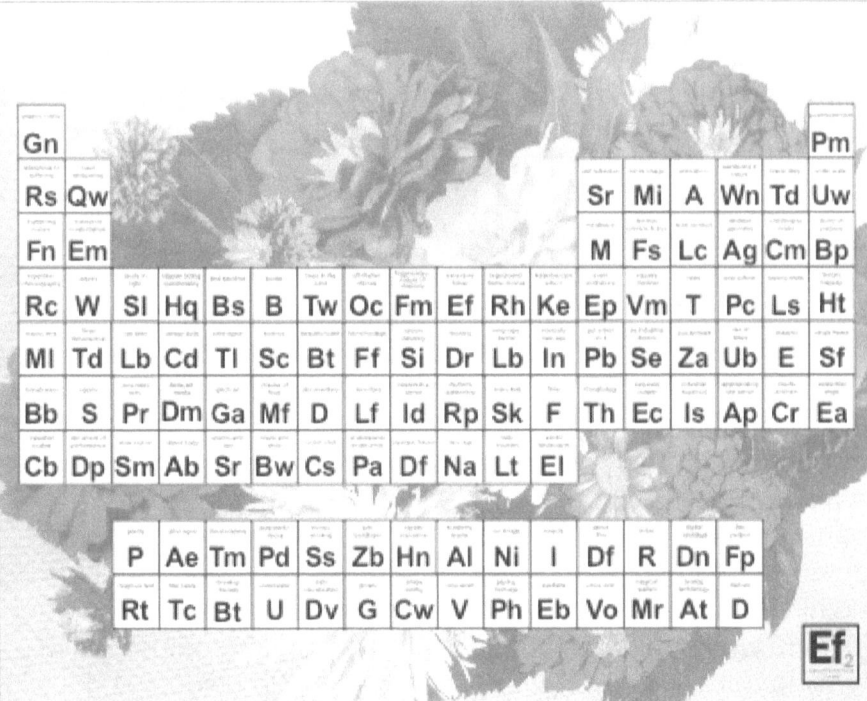

Periodic Table of the Elements of Experimental Film

EFF**Portland 2013**

Experimental Film Festival Portland

May 20 - 26

www.effportland.com
#effpdx13

presented by: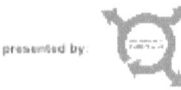

 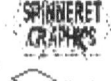 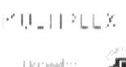 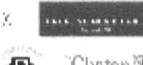 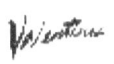 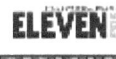

 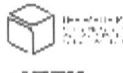   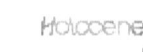

 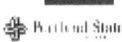   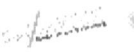

unto itself. All in all, the hope was to bring back to life the experimental film community that people had always talked about thriving in Portland, and I believe we had succeeded!

I have currently stepped aside from the film festival, while still working to enable folks to obtain screenings here in Portland who might be stopping through. The combination of large-scale curating, making my own films, and the ol' day job, has given me pause. The communities that I have been a part of and have helped to build will always make me smile, and I hope to one day return to it on the same level. But as I write this, I feel I must concentrate on other aspects of life. I hope for others who have experienced communities similar to what I have participated in, the one we built here, to be jumping up and down at the chance to put a microcinema together. There is nothing like these small-scale groups who desire to screen not just the works they have made, but also bring together those who do not have the chance to see their own unique works with an audience. There's nothing like it. And while part of me can get bitter thinking about the natural art world relations (ego) which come with the territory, I wish for more of these types of screenings, fests, and dedicated spaces to continue forth with bold open arms to those who are interested in creating alternative forms of media. For in a world where the media so largely controls the thoughts, actions and psychology of the masses, it is noble and good to create environments which work to dispel the notion that there is only one type of filmmaking, or only one voice.

About the Artist

Ben Popp is a filmmaker, educator and curator living in Portland Oregon. He is currently the media education coordinator at Portland Community Media and teaches animation on the side to both young kids and adults.

Eye Contact

By: Kristen Lauth Shaeffer

Just over two years ago, I became a parent. Having a baby certainly impacted how I managed my time and made creative work, and I found that one way to continue creating was to incorporate my family into the process. When my daughter was nine months old, she and I experienced our first collaboration in a piece entitled camerawork cameraplay. In the film, my daughter and I both operate cameras (hers, a child's toy video camera) simultaneously recording one another. The short edited piece is a split screen of our footage synced with one another. It was a meaningful experience for me to shoot something with her; she loved chewing on the camera.

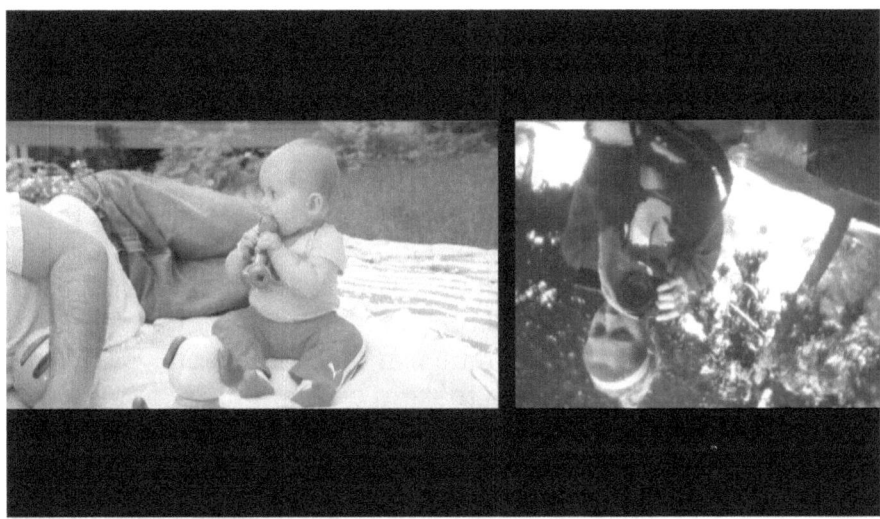

Still From *Camerawork Cameraplay* (2013) By Kristen Lauth Shaeffer

Independent/un-dependent film and videomakers understand the conventions of film and choose to challenge them. Because of our independence, we can explore ideas in unusual ways. The resulting work may not have a place in a traditional or major film festival; the film may not "fit." Independent/un-dependent film festivals give us filmmakers a place to exhibit work and a way to engage in dialogue with an audience. My experiment, camerawork cameraplay, screened publicly thanks to un-dependent festivals including Experiments in Cinema v9.72 in 2014. The shared experience with my daughter became a shared experience with others.

One could argue that the Internet is a place for independent and experimental work to be exhibited, and in many ways, it is. I myself eventually put all of my work online because I'd rather my work be seen than not. But I know that this type of viewing experience is not the same as a festival screening. An online screening means that the viewer may be distracted by email and advertisements and cat videos in neighboring browser windows. We all spend a lot of time with the Internet; we know what this feels like.

Attending an independent festival screening is a thoughtful, intentional choice. It's a decision that requires making time and arrangements, not an impulsive click of a link because there are a few minutes to kill. In this kind of experience, the audience will sit in a dark space and watch your film; it will essentially be the only thing in their field of vision and the only thing that they hear. During this kind of experience, it's as if you and the viewer are making eye contact in your conversation. From my perspective as a filmmaker, this moment is amazing; I think it's why many of us pursue film and video work. Creating work independently gives us makers an opportunity to say what is not being said elsewhere, and we need a place to say it.

Festivals that program our work allow us to have these intimate "conversations" with people who want to make the time to have them. (Of course as our film screens we lose some control, as the viewer will create his or her own meaning, but that's a magic part of the whole process, too.) And if we're lucky, the conversations will continue after everyone leaves the theater. From my perspective as a viewer, we need these festivals for these experiences; it seems like the best way to have them. So many of us desire to be challenged, and we want to hear from minority and unheard voices in film and video. I appreciate when a mediamaker gives me enough credit as an audience member that they leave me to interpret what I hear and see for myself. I want to be an active participant in the experience. I want to make eye contact in the conversation.

My daughter is now a toddler. A few days ago we had a moment that led me to pick up our copy of Dr. Spock's Baby and Childcare. As I was reading a passage about "being two," I somehow got sidetracked by a section of the book that's about the media. So in my concluding thoughts, I reference not a filmmaker or film theorist, but rather the author of one of the country's oldest and best-known childcare books, Benjamin Spock, M.D.

Dr. Spock writes that media (particularly television, but the idea could be generalized) has "a tendency to promote passivity and a lack of creativity" (738). He states that it "requires little mental activity on the viewer's part," and that "you simply sit and let the images flow by" (738). His perspective states that media is harmful for children, and perhaps everyone.

"You simply sit and let the images flow by." It seems to me that this description is not at all accurate regarding what we see in an independent or experimental festival. From a film's creation, to the festival's programming, to the audience's viewing, each step of the process is active and challenging. Each step inspires creativity and engagement.

As my daughter gets older, I hope that she'll have access to independent/un-dependent media through festivals. I hope that she'll view film and video as a way to convey ideas and to engage in meaningful dialogue, whatever her interests may be. I hope that she'll choose to be an active participant. At the very least, I hope that she'll do a little more than chew on that video camera.

About the Artist

Kristen Lauth Shaeffer lives and creates in Pittsburgh, Pennsylvania, where she is an Assistant Professor of Film and Digital Technology at Chatham University. Her short films have screened at Experiments in Cinema, Athens International Film + Video Festival, Big Muddy Film Festival, Dallas VideoFest and others. She is particularly interested in creating work around themes of family, identity, and community.

Reference

Spock, Benjamin, and Robert Needlman. Dr. Spock's Baby and Child Care. New York: Gallery, 2012. Print.

Cinema, *redivivus*

By: Tina Wasserman

As the nineteenth century came to a close, the remarkable art of cinema emerged. Across continents inventors such as Thomas Edison in the United States and the Lumière brothers in France had been working to sequence static photographic images into the illusion of cinematic movement. Edison's inventive instinct was to build a mechanism that would attract individual viewers. What emerged was the Kinetoscope, a viewing device in which a single person could observe short cinematic vignettes through an optical lens placed on the top of a large cabinet. Inside the boxed structure, serialized photographic stills printed onto looped bands of perforated and flexible strips were electronically pulled across spools and sprockets, thus producing the illusion of movement. After the first Kinetoscope parlor opened in New York City, on Broadway in 1894, Edison's moving image machines were an immediate success.

But another viewing process that was being developed by the Lumière brothers almost simultaneously eclipsed Edison's method. The device they invented, the Cinématographe, not only recorded and printed cinematic images, but also projected them on to a screen. When the Lumière Brothers famously organized the first public screening of their work on December 28, 1895, at the Salon Indien du Grand Café in Paris, the cinema, as art form of projected moving images, was born. For much of the following century, cinema would be a collectively viewed art form and the experience of it would be public and simultaneously shared.

The seventh art thus emerged as a formidable force on to the twentieth-century stage. An emblem of the age of industry and invention, its large and collective format would profoundly transform the very fabric of modern experience and indeed would become a symbol of both the problems and possibilities of modernity itself. Some critics of the new medium were horrified by its escapist power to seduce and sedate. German sociologist Siegfried Kracauer accused the Weimar populace of being addicted to distraction in their devotion to the movies shown at the large picture palaces of Berlin in the 1920s. But others, like the cultural theorist Walter Benjamin were more hopeful that the large mass audiences attracted to cinema meant it had the potential to be a fully democratized art form. To all, it was clear that this new medium both influenced and was used to influence a wide range of ideologies and cultural practices. From the politics of the Soviet avant-garde to the escapist entertainment of Hollywood, cinema was recognized as a powerful mechanism for mass communication.

But as we head deeper into the twenty-first century, the character of this collective, public medium and art form, so essential to the popular and political life of the twentieth century has inevitably changed into new formats. Having shrunk and splintered into the multiplex, then migrated onto television's privatized and smaller screen, it has finally miniaturized into our singular and portable digital devices. The moving images of cinema, once mythic, communal and large, have indeed reverted back to their Edison origins.

While it is true that moving images are everywhere and all around us, our reception of this ultra-mediated world has increasingly become private and individuated. There may be two billion viewings posted on the latest online video, but that count is tabulated from the multiplicity of isolated views. As collective spectatorship erodes, moving image culture becomes less a shared and public experience than a mass of individuated views of the same–increasingly generic–global data.

This is why the work of the experimental film festival has become so important. For it is not just within the experimental film community where one finds some of the most compelling challenges to the limits of film language and subject matter expressed, but also where one finds the deepest desire to preserve cinema's history, particularly as the medium transforms from its photochemical past toward its increasingly digital future. A large part of this preservation is predicated on the desire to maintain the public and collective experience of cinema as an art form of projected moving images. The experimental film festival ensures that the visual exuberance of the cinematic image can be fully experienced in communally shared time and space. With its live-ness, its bringing together of local, national, and global film communities and work, its attention to contemporary experimental practices and to the history of the projected image, the experimental film festival points toward future moving image practices while maintaining an archive of cinema's history. Although numerous festivals devote some of their programming to older celluloid formats, in many projection has become mostly digital. While we may no longer see the beam of light falling out of the projection booth, or the sound of the projector gates transporting strips of cinema through sprockets, shutters, light, and lenses, these technologies have become the raw material for new experimental, para-cinematic work—often performed at experimental film festivals and elsewhere—that recycles and repurposes past cinematic apparatuses. The machine age of a public and projected cinema may be waning, but in preserving its practices, experimental filmmakers and festivals embrace its memory and the art of cinema is revived.

About the Artist

Tina Wasserman has a Ph.D in Cinema Studies and teaches in the Visual and Critical Studies Department at The School of the Museum of Fine Arts, Boston.

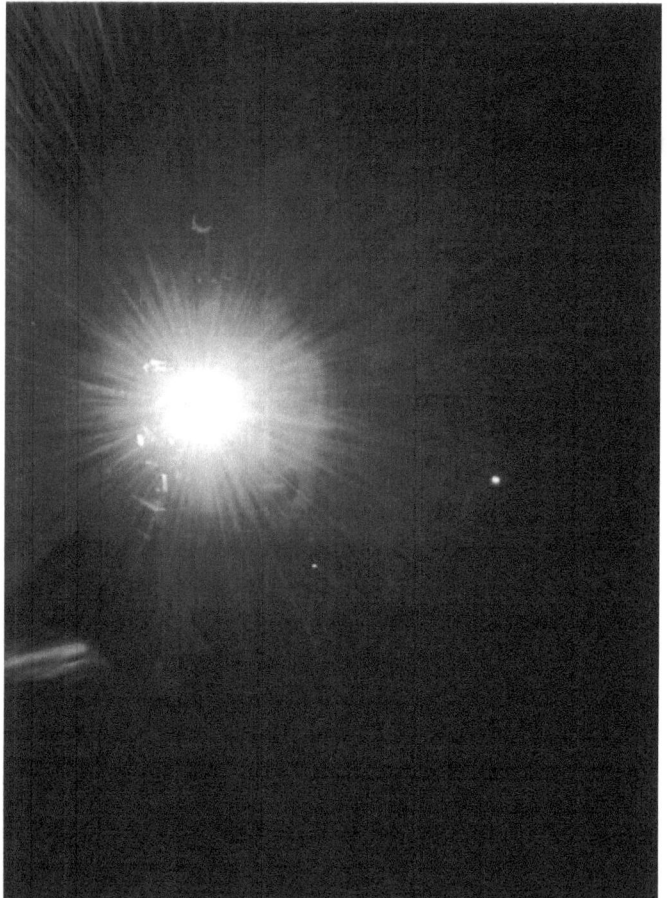

Photograph of live projection show by Tina Wasserman

"Don't Even *Look* At It" - Pixelvision & Multi-Screens

By: Gerry Fialka

Intrigued by the words "Don't even look at it" which appear now on the big screen as an attempt by movie theaters to control cellphone use, I'd like to explore how social media is changing the viewing experience at public film screenings. These days, audience members literally cup their hands during screenings to peek at their phone. At my film screenings, I announce: "We have decided to watch one big screen for the next few hours. Please use other screens in the other room." It seems that many can't watch the one big screen unless they can directly access their personal screen during that two hour period. Human inventions (whether tangible or not) have services and disservices. We look to the artists to reveal inventions' hidden effects on our psyche. This can help us cope. While we use the term "media" to mean many things, at its broadest, media can be defined as "any human invention."

Artist Stan VanDerBeek (1927-1984) asserted that people can take in, associate and categorize an excess of simultaneous imagery. He noticed in 1961 that artists were "abandoning the logics of aesthetics, springing full blown into a juxtaposed and simultaneous world that ignores the one-point-perspective mind."

Media, in this context, constitutes new environments, which can have profound impacts on us. We can survey each new invention and, by reflecting on them, learn to turn breakdowns into breakthroughs. For example, one subliminal effect of cars is the enhancement of private mobility. I drove 45 minutes to a job for ten years, and found this period to be calming. The autopilot mode spurred contemplation, which could be considered a service. The disservices of cars are well known.

As in the automobile example there is a tendency to cast judgment, but judging the effects of media can block the comprehensive understanding of them. To emphasize the benefit of "suspended judgment," Marshall McLuhan suggested, "Understanding is *not* having a point of view." Due to the fractured nature of life immersed in a multi-screen environment, how can we wholly analyze its individual and cumulative effects? We might consider the motives and consequences of its trailblazers: Abel Gance, the 1939 NY World's Fair, Canada's Labyrinth Pavilion - Expo '67, the ONCE Group, Harry Smith, and Nam June Paik. "Frame within frame" variations were advanced by Hollis Frampton, Peter Greenaway, and James Wickstead, with his invention of Pixelvsion. More innovators include: Charles & Ray Eames, Agnes Varda, John & James Whitney, Andy Warhol, Ken Jacobs, Chris Marker, Edmund Carpenter, Walter Alter, Scott Stark, Doug Aitken and Christian Marclay, with his "vertical editing."

Even Richard Nixon and Elvis watched many TVs at once. Lounging before a wall of televisions, David Bowie's character in Nicolas Roeg's *The Man Who Fell to Earth* was depicted at his most de- bauched and degraded moment, iconically representing the psychic instability that Roeg imagined to be innate to the multi-screen environment.
How can we navigate the stream of sensory overload into channels of continuity that enable human evolution (vs. the discontinuity of devolution)?

Facebook, YouTube, electronic billboards, GPS, and computers are omnipresent. What does submersion among so many screens—all the time—do to us? "The multiplicity-of-the-media experience we have today will alienate people from identifying with any medium. So people will finally get detached from the hypnotic effect of each medium." This 2008 forecast of Robert Dobbs suggests the redemption of humanity from alienating experience will follow on its own, naturally and inevitably. The idea is that the individual and social mind will become sophisticated in due time and regain possession of itself. Can "media multiplicity" *as* an art form itself create the collective consciousness of today? How?

Tactile Situation Awareness (TSA) refers to the act of pilots acting so fast, there's no time to really read data and respond accordingly. They focus on the center of the cyclone. Likewise, we are engulfed in sensorial whirlpools. Can we ever *really* get *deeply* involved? For self-preservation, we cannot really specialize and truly see *one* screen. Or can we?

Does all this make you want to come out and play? The word "play" comes from the Old English "plegan," which means "move rapidly, occupy or busy oneself, exercise; frolic; make sport of, mock; perform music." *Let's rock on sum funkey music.* Fun is the key. *Free your mind and your mockin' essay will follow.*

Let's play around like Bob Fosse, as detailed in the book *Fosse* by Sam Wasson, who wrote that his dancers seemed "as if they were playing at dancing more than actually dancing." Let's play at playing. Jimi Hendrix said, "You've got to have a purpose in life. But I'm not here to talk, I'm here to play." Miles Davis encouraged "Play what you don't know."

All art aspires to the condition of music. Like an all-encompassing environment, it's a center without margins. Can you tell the dance from the dancer? The scream from the screen? The essay from the writer?

Aren't our eyes doing what the multi-screen phenomenon demands of them anyway? *Awake thee as actors in the global theater, and let's party.* To better illustrate what I am *not* trying to say, but sing and dance, let's talk "Pixelvision" aka "PXL." We can turn the limitations of this toy video camera into strengths, and reshape "undependent filmmaking," a term I first heard from comrade Bryan Konefsky. I feel that his clarion call encourages unlearning and reinventing.

PXL challenges us to participate in the multi-screen environment by becoming aware of it simply by playing along. When the live vaudeville show dominated the theater-going experience, the earliest films were called "chasers." Theater owners used them with the intent to clear the hall and replace one audience with a new round of paying customers. They would put on a film, which would chase the audience out. PXL, as I've found, is similar in effect and potential.

In the 80's, I was working as an archivist for Frank Zappa. When the notorious LA press kitten Cindy Lamb showed Frank the PXL camera, he was intrigued. That's how I first learned about PXL.

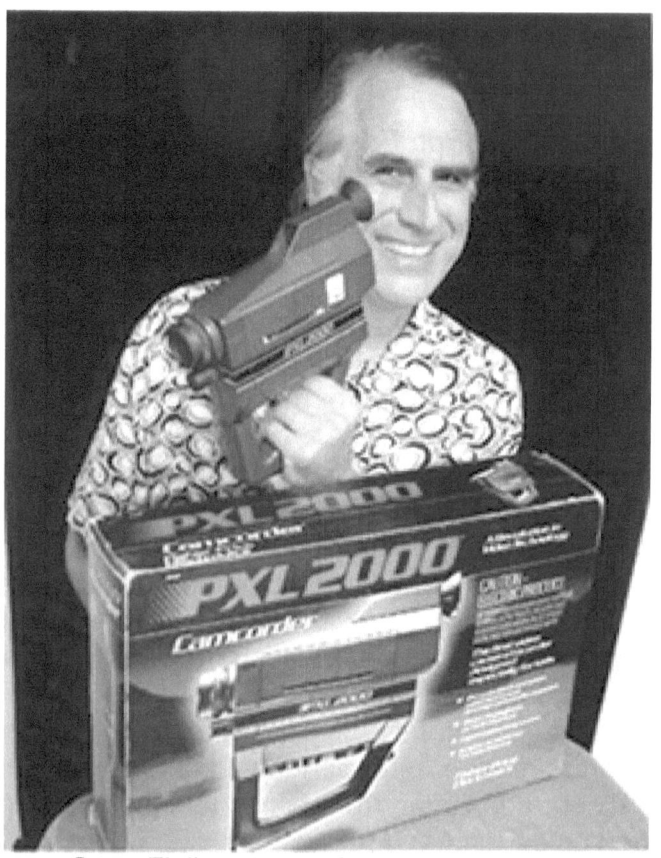

Gerry Fialka with his favorite toy camera

Inspired by his satirical subversion and an article on PXL in *Mondo 2000*, I started the PXL THIS Film Festival in 1991. As a put-on artist, who puts on events, this genuine fake film festival, is a way of seeing the paradoxical exuberance of being through electronic folk art. The potential thrills of PXL THIS lure people to see it, and occasionally, they run out screaming, "It sucks. It's black & white, and looks crappy. I can't even look at it!" Preeminent avant-garde filmmaker James Benning, who says, "I like toys," was in our first festival with *Table Top*. He captured an inherent uniqueness of Pixelvision by utilizing the end-of-the-tape glitch. Since PXL records picture and sound on an audiocassette, this glitchiness could be considered a limitation. Lisa Marr's *Rugrat* (2004) keenly utilized another PXL innate characteristic by miming the pixel's blocky graininess with the patterns of Navajo rugs.

Village Voice critic J. Hoberman, who wrote years ago, "PXL is the ultimate people's video," presaged *The Hollywood Reporter,* who recently called it the "precursor of today's DV filmmaking."

The toy company Fisher Price manufactured 400,000 of these lovable plastic toy wonders from 1987 to 1989. The irresistible irony of the PXL 2000 is that the camera's ease-of-use and afforda- bility, which democratizes movie making, inspires the creation of some of the most visionary, avant and luminous films of our time. Since 1987, PXL cameras have sometimes cost as little as 5 bucks.

Though its prices have ranged from the original sticker price of $100 to more over the years, they still can be found. In fact, Patrick Gill of bentstruments.com can repair and modify them. *Get off your ass and PXL.*

As we bathe in the glossy techno-freaked swirl of today's culture, swimming in the warm glow of Pixelvision reimagines the gothic dreamy look of the old black and white classics. In

IFP Magazine, Ethan Hawke said during an interview about making Michael Almereyda's *Hamlet,* that the director loved using a camera from "the 50's." It was the PXL-2000, a timeless artifact for everyone. The noir look evokes Billy Wilder, who claims that black-and-white is more true than color.

"If movies offer an escape from everyday life, Pixelvision is the Houdini of the film world," noted a *SF Weekly* reviewer. One of my personal heroes, George Manupelli, founder of the Ann Arbor Film Festival, filmmaker, poet, and environmental activist, nailed it best when he said, "When the aliens are here and deciding whether to vaporize all mankind for our inhumanity, cruelty and greed, showing the aliens PXL THIS will save the world. PXL THIS shows our best nature as humanist creators and subversives against those who deserve it. Save the world. Support PXL THIS."

PXL THIS has screened a wide range of innovators:
Lee Ranaldo (Sonic Youth), Chris Metzler (*Fishbone* and *Salton Sea* documentaries), James & Sadie Benning, Joe Gibbons, Cecilia Dougherty, Peggy Ahwesh, Jesse Drew, Margie Strosser, Cory McAbee (*The Billy Nayer Show*), Terri Sarris, Bryan Konefsky, Geoff Seelinger, LM Sabo, Will Erokan, Clint Enns, Paul Bacca, Clifford Novey and tENTATIVELY a cONVENIENCE. Pixelvision has made it onto the big screen via Richard Linklater *(Slacker),* Michael Almereyda (*Nadja, Hamlet* & many more), and Craig Baldwin (*Sonic Outlaws*). PXL THIS has been attended by Oliver Stone, Daryl Hannah, Kim Fowley among others.

PXL THIS is the second oldest film festival in Los Angeles. Celebrating "cinema povera" and electronic Pointillism, it evokes Marcel Duchamp's axiom, "Poor tools require better skills." However, I'd say that one can make moving image art *both* with professional and primitive tools. We shape our tools, and then they shape us. *The New York Times* called PXL THIS "small." Many of our most inspiring entries come from Venice,

California's Board- walk performers and homeless people. *I am every- day peoplePXL.*

Like Rube Goldberg, Pixelators create an unassuming addition to our throw-away culture. These low- tech, hi-jinx films reconfigure conventional cinema language. Denny Moynahan (aka King Kukulele) has performed with his PXL-self for over 15 years evoking the "live performance cinema" of Winsor McCay, Buster Keaton and Pat Oleszko.

McLuhan said, "If it works, it's obsolete." One audience member said that with all the great new digital effects and equipment, it seems as though you could "fix" the picture. PXL is remarkable because it does not work. Yet, in 2014, PXL THIS celebrated twenty four years, which proves wrong this quote by PXL pioneer Erik Saks: "Pixelvison is an aberrant art form, underscored by the fact that since the cameras wear out quickly, and are no longer being manufactured, it holds within itself authorized obsolescence. Each time an artist uses a PXL 2000, the whole form edges closer to extinction." *Ain't no stopping us now. Dig infinity...focus.*

PXL enables us to embrace the contradictions of its services and disservices as a failed toy *and* a successful art-making device. The *LA Weekly* contrasted it as "a tool for creativity *and* adolescent regression." Film critic Amy Taubin says: "Artists want to do things that break the rules of the mainstream. Just picking up a PXL 2000 camcorder is breaking a kind of rule about what an image should look like." Artists try to evoke children's innocence. So why not just start out with a kid's toy? The Balinese have no word for art; they do everything as well as they can. Try this joke: A kid comes of age when he realizes his Dad goes to work. The kid asks his Dad, "What is your job?" His Dad, an art teacher, responds, "I teach people how to draw." Kid says, "You mean they forgot?"

Filmmakers and educators Lisa Marr and Paolo Davanzo have made PXL shorts for many years. Their Echo Park Film Center, who rents PXL camcorders, nurtures our same ideals - to gather the community to share in the creative process via connectedness not consumerism. We hoick up an ecstatic new state of tribal immediacy and simultaneity.

Echo Park Film Center and Craig Baldwin of OtherCinema have programmed the PXL THIS Film Festival at their acclaimed venues dozens of times. Steve Polta booked PXL THIS at the prestigious San Francisco Cinematheque. The program notes, entitled *An Invention Without A Future - Pixelvision: Electronic Folk Art*, comprehensively documents the history of PXL THIS and Pixelvision. More essential reading is Andrea Nina McCarthy's 2005 MIT thesis *Toying With Obsoles- cence: Pixelvision Filmmakers & The Fisher Price PXL 2000 Camera.*

PXL THIS Film Festival has no awards and no entry fees. Out of 2 to 3 dozen entries per year, we show every entry. They have come from across the US, France, Canada, England and New Zealand. Stalwart Pixelator Doug Ing has contributed PXL camcorders to the new wave of young filmmakers like Chester Burnett, whose witty films have been an audience favorite since he as a child.

T. S. Eliot said that poetry is outing your inner dialogue. What form is your inner dialogue in? Maybe it's that dreamy illusive Pixelvision image. An extension of consciousness? The next medium? The non-physical? The possibility of a world without words? The PXL viewer sees less information (2,000 dots instead of regular TV's 200,000) and gets more involved. Low definition means high participation. The PXL mosaic reimagines Seurat-like bits of information moving at the speed of light.

What is faster - the speed of light or the speed of thought? Hang in there as I free-associate. May I suggest a funky out-jazz guitar solo, metaphorically speaking?

Standing on the verge of PXLing on. In the very midst of this funkathon rave party, it's time to imagine Eddie Hazel and Michael Hampton (better yet, Sonny Sharrock and Pete Cosey) shredding cosmic verbiage to access the unconsciousness. Eliot influenced the Symbolists, who promoted that it's not so much what you say, but how it makes you feel. Mallarmé exhorted, "Don't paint the thing, paint the effect it produces." McLuhan said, "Multi- screen projection tends to end the story-line, as the symbolist poem ends narrative in verse."

Let's enliven the "content and form" in surveying the subliminal effects of Pixelvision, multiple screens, and essays in film festival books with more:

In *Film Culture Reader* (1970), P. Adams Sitney included Annette Michelson's essay *Film and the Radical Aspiration*. Here's an excerpt:

> "In a country whose power and affluence are maintained by the dialectic of a war economy, in a country whose dream of revolution has been sublimated in reformism and frustrated by an equivocal prosperity, cinematic radicalism is condemned to a politics and strategy of social and aesthetic subversion.
>
> 'To live,' as Webern, quoting Hö lderlin, said, 'is to defend a form.' It is from the strength of its forms that cinema's essential power of negation, its 'liquidation of traditional elements in our culture,' as Benjamin put it, will derive and sustain its cathartic power.
>
> Within the structure of our culture, ten-year-olds are now filming 8mm serials—mostly science fiction, I am told—in

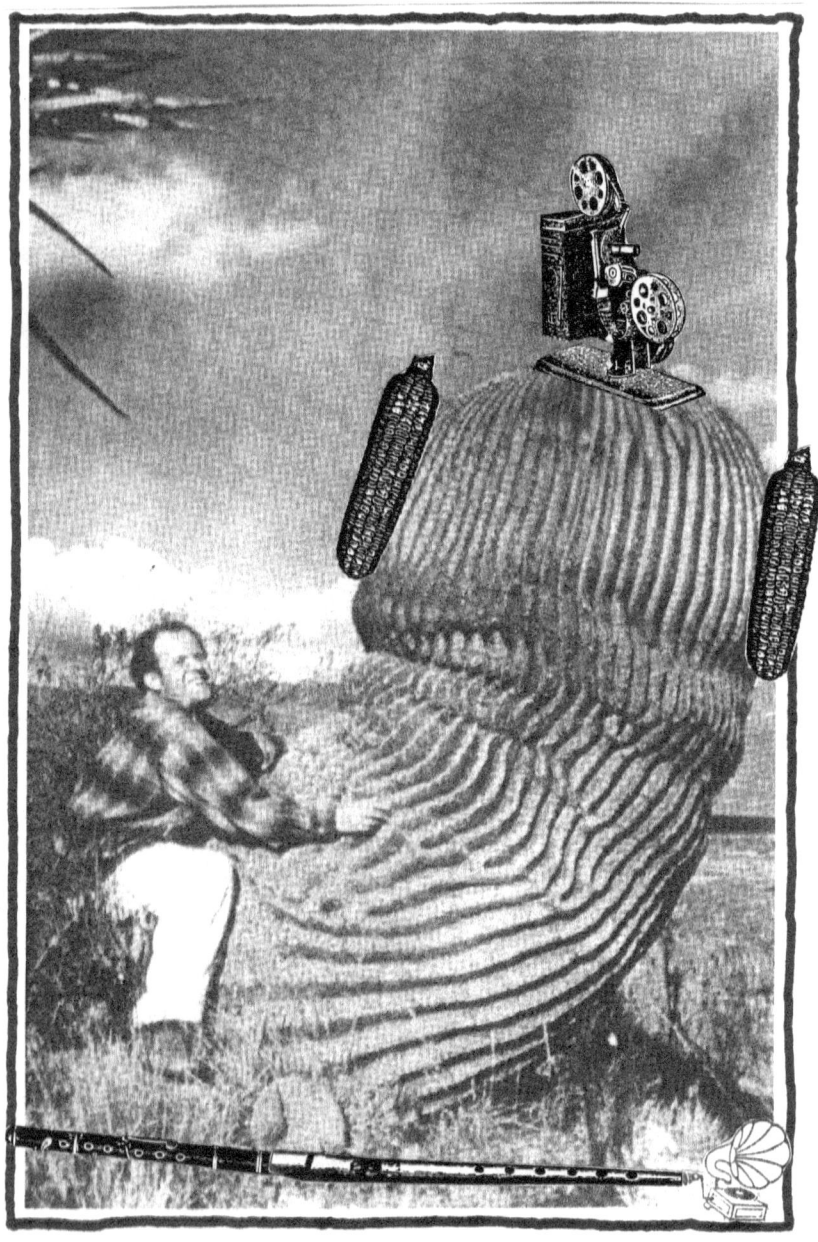

Gerry Fialka

"Noise Floor - Sergei Eisenstein in Mexico, 1930. Photographer Unknown."
Collage by Gerry Fialka

their own backyards. This perhaps is the *single most interesting fact* about cinema. Given this new accessibility of the medium, anything can happen.

Astruc's dream of the camera as fountain pen is transcended, the camera becomes a toy, and the element of play is restored to cinematic enterprise. One thinks of Méliès, both Child and Father of cinema, and one rejoices in the promise of his reincarnation in the generation of little Americans making science-fiction films after school in those backyards. Here, I do believe, lies the excitement of cinema's future, its ultimate radical potential. And as André Breton, now a venerable radical, has said, 'The work of art is valid if, and only if, it is aquiver with a sense of the future.'"

Michelson presages Pixelvision effects. She refers to Alexandre Astruc's 1948 article *The Birth of a New Avant-Garde: La Camera-Stylo* which probes the arrival of a new period in the development of cinema when the medium could be as flexible as a simple fountain pen. PXL hoicks up pen-and-paper mentality. It enables one to utilize intuition by reimaging everydayness into utter profundity. One viewer told me how it's amazing that a PXL film can look silly, but be profound. If the maker tries to be profound, it does not work.

Tony Conrad wanted to make a film that stimulates what things look like with one's eyes closed. He said the role of the artist is to break laws that have not been made yet. *Jump back and kiss your PXL.*

Bucky Fuller's "It is literally possible to do more with less" reminds me of two Jean Cocteau quotes: "Film will become art when its materials are as inexpensive as pencil and paper," and "What one should do with the young is to give them a portable camera and forbid them to observe any rules except those they invent for themselves as they go along. Let them write without being afraid of making mistakes."

Let's continue these fiery discussions so we may study the hidden psychic effects of hybridizing a light-through medium (TV, stained glass windows, video, computer screens) and a light-on medium (film, the printed word, murals). And continue to study nothing. With how shitty Pixelvision can sometimes look, I have found the audience staring at a blank screen. That's McLuhan's "Media Fast." That's sustainability, aka "Media Ecology," which is being aware of an organism and its environment. I started out with nothing and still have most of it left. "A true Zen saying, 'Nothing is what I want.'" - Zappa.

The poet Auden posed the question: do we really know if art activates or pacifies us? Marx said the point is to change the world, not interpret it. You can't change shit, Karl, our inventions change us. The telegraph caused the civil war (how can you ever have a "civil" war?), and the radio caused WWII. If we combine this technological determinism *with* Menippean satire, we can learn how *not* to ignore the hidden psyche effects of our inventions. Bingo. We can *cope*.

The hottest new study topic is cognitive neuroscience. Everything we invent extends some human sensorium: clothing extends skin, knife and fork extends teeth, film editing extends the eye lid (blinking), and the film viewing experience extends memory. "As if a magic lantern threw the nerves in patterns on a screen" - T.S. Eliot, *The Love Song of J. Alfred Prufrock*. Pudovkin claims, "The film is the greatest teacher because it teaches us not only through the brain but through the whole body."

Ponder the intentions behind our inventions. Sydney Lumet said films can't cause anything, but that won't keep him from trying. Warhol said, "It's the movies that have really been running things in America ever since they were invented. They show you what to do, how to do it, when to do it, how to feel about it, and how to look how you feel about it." Reagan went into the White House after his in- auguration and asked, "Where's the war room?" He was referring to what he heard in the Stanley Ku- brick film *Dr. Strangelove*, with the infamous line "There will be no fighting in the war room!"

As for Stan the Man, Kubrick pulled *A Clockwork Orange* for three decades from *only* UK screens. When the British police suggested copycats inspired by his film could target his family, did he pull the film as PR strategy or was he truly scared? Did he *actually* believe his film could cause crimes?

Poet Richard Modiano told me the movies can catalyze fashion trends like James Dean wearing a white T-shirt. Gillo Pontecorvo, whose *The Battle of Al- giers* was used as a training film for the Black Panthers *and* Bush's cronies, was asked what his film does to people. He said that it teaches them how to make films. In 1924, D.W. Griffith proclaimed "In the year 2024 the most important single thing that the cinema will have helped in a large way to accomplish will be that of eliminating from the face of the civilized world all armed conflict."

Brother Gene Youngblood, can you paradigm? He wrote in 1970, "The nature of cinema (is) so encompassing and persuasive that it promises to dominate all image-making in much the same way as the theory of general relativity dominates all physics." What *are* the services and disservices of the current multi-screen dominance and low-tech filmmaking? *Get the funk outta disfunktional.*

Unintended consequences can be flipped into services by understanding the relationships of the human invention and "the user as content." When McLuhan quipped, "Culture is our business," he hoped to invigorate the needling of that

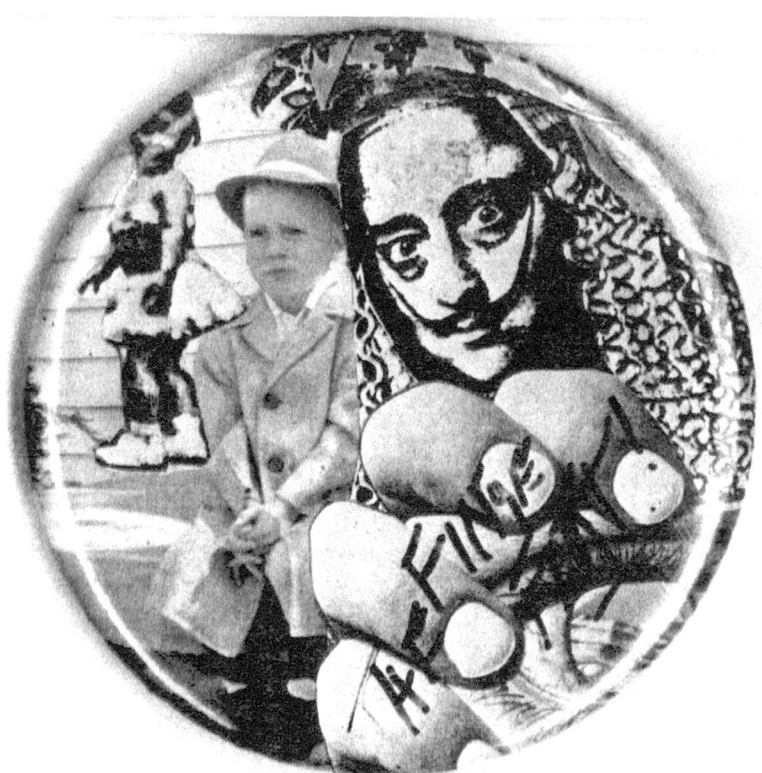

Finger Fart - Silent But Deadly – collage by Gerry Fialka, lettering by
Timothy Agoglia Carey, 1974

somnambulistic state that all inventions cause. We embrace
them before we even study what they do to us. In fact, can we
ever learn that the real hidden ground to all of this is electricity?
I can relate to Charles Ives, who said, "Music—that no one
knows what it is—and the less he knows he knows what it is
the nearer it is to music— probably."
And, yes, "probably" I should drop this following "failure" rant.
Maybe this mosaic mash-up of PXL and multi-screens is a
Menippean satirized metaphor of me, doing the multiplicity
mambo.

I may be a failure at this essay, but I am not a miserable failure.
This mumbo jumbo jes grew. A last ditch attempt to gain

credibility? Nah, maybe just another carny poser snake-oiling loopy slapstick to avoid the elusive bitch goddess of success. So carefully make plans, and then do the opposite.

Why do we *ignore* the hidden effects?

"Communication of the new is a miracle, but not impossible." - McLuhan, who loved Sam Goldwyn's "As for the critics, don't even ignore them." Initiate conversations on the resonating interval, sense ratio shifting, effects precede causes, and kaleidoscopic synesthesia. In Marcel Duchampian spirit, start a film festival that is not a film festival. Write the mosaic aphoristic gestalt into a living organism. Explode the experiments with the unexpected.

This essay has been formatted to fit your discarnate body. It hoicks up Wyndham Lewis as articulated by McLuhan: "Lewis sought no disciples, nor does he offer a program or solution, rather his contribution is a critical discipline. Lewis is a stimulant, a mode of perception, rather than a position or practice."

Don't even *look* at *this*?

And in the tradition of ReSearch Publications, here's more quotes and probes:
"Artists live in the present and write a detailed history of the future" - Wyndham Lewis, who taught McLuhan that human inventions are teaching machines. Awake people and continue this tradition of all-at-onceness, which was made explicit by Dziga Vertov in his landmark modernist film, *Man With The Movie Camera* (1929). Ricky Leacock aspired to make films that make you feel present.

Richard Linklater voiced "Everything is now" in *Boyhood*. Alan Watts yelped "Time is always now. Groove with the eternal now." Let's boogaloo with Baba Ram Dass - "Be Here Now." *All times are happening now!*

"The next medium—whatever it is—may be an extension of consciousness. It will include television as its content, not as its environment, and will transform television into an art form." - McLuhan.

This evokes Edgar Allen Poe's reasoning backwards. He invented the detective novel. "Anything that's popular is a rear-view image" - McLuhan.

Study anthropologist Gregory Bateson's Double Bind Theory - pay no attention to me that I am lying to you. We do it with ourselves all the time. It is similar to James Benning saying that the film viewing audience has a contract with themselves to sit for two hours. David Sherman suggested that we may be making a Faustian bargain. How much does it really matter if you're watching one screen or many?

"And here the word 'experimental' is apt, providing it is understood not as descriptive of an act to be later judged in terms of success or failure, but simply as of an act the outcome of which is unknown or not foreseen." - John Cage Contemplate this McLuhan question: "How about technologies as the collective unconscious and art as the collective unconsciousness?" And then, Zappa's quiz: "Who are the brain police?"

Getting down just for the funk of it, United Muta- tions! One cybernation under a groove.

McLuhan extended Mallarmé's "To define is to kill, to suggest is to create" to "evolution is to adapting to exploration."
Take the opportunity to actually read, study and discuss McLuhan, Joyce & Robert Dobbs. Delve deep into McLuhan's translation of *Finnegans Wake* by James Joyce, who invented

Facebook and disguised it as a book. Dobbs' translation of them both transforms and reinvents percept plunder for the recent future.

Research the books of Janine Marchessault, who wrote about The Labyrinth Project's lasting effect: "One can see in the expanded screen experiments at Expo a foreshadowing of the intermedia, and the concomitant multiplication of screens in everyday life and around the world."

Seminal experimental filmmaker Hollis Frampton questioned "suspended judgment" in 1978: "I didn't really like the work I thought was my best work. I liked the stuff I didn't like a lot more."

Special thanks to Suzy Williams, Matt Collins, Mark Hardin, Derek Gibb, Jules Minton, River Quane and Here Comes Everybody. Everything they wanted me to add or delete, I meant to. "Everybody is a star." – Sly Stone.

About the Artist

Artist, writer, and paramedia ecologist lectures world-wide on experimental film, avant-garde art and subversive social media. He has curated three film series in LA for over three decades. Fialka has been praised by the Los Angeles Times as "the multi-media Renais- sance man." The LA Weekly proclaimed him "a cultural revolutionary."

On Scorpios, Leather (and Satin) Jackets and the Importance of Experimental Film Festivals
By: Kamila Kuc

It has been a while since I attended a film festival. In the past I visited many festivals, mainly as press, curator, and jury member. Most of these festivals have now transformed themselves into multi-faceted industry events, with carefully pre-planned, strategy-oriented business meetings. The VIP lounges and parties that require the most in vogue outfits; cine-markets, pitching sessions, talent markets—these are all part of what is no doubt an exciting overall experience. More often than not, however, these sideshow elements and events seem more important than the actual film screenings. It is such vulture-like money-oriented investor's approach to film (even though, naturally, one recognizes the necessity for filmmakers and producers to engage with such activities) that prompted filmmakers like Gregory Markopoulos to gradually withdraw from the film world. In 2013, being familiar with most of the key European festivals in France, Germany, and the UK, I was more than happy to accept an invitation to the somewhat less known Alternative Film/Video Festival in Belgrade, Serbia, to give a presentation on Polish avant-garde film as part of their annual Academic Forum. Curiously, as stimulating as the Academic Forum was, that year's Festival turned out to have had little to do with my academic participation… A couple of entries from my 'Alternative Film and Video Notebook' should illustrate this.

****

12 December (Thursday), 2013. Alternative Film and Video. Belgrade, Serbia.

I made it to Michelle Mellor's and Bryan Konefsky's 16mm Loop Making Workshop as part of the Experiments in Cinema Festival (New Mexico) presented at the Alternative Film/Video this year. I rushed from my hotel in Stari Grad (Old Belgrade) to arrive in the room just in time to catch the glimpse of Bruce Conner's *Marilyn Times Five* (1968 – 1973). We were asked to select a roll of film from a pile on the floor. I had forgotten how it feels to touch film; its smell; 'the vinegar syndrome.' Much to my surprise, the film of my blind choice was educational colour footage about the Hopi Indians. I have an extensive interest in Native American culture and in my high school years back in Poland I was a member of an international activist group called 'Freedom for Leonard Peltier.' Moreover, on my first night in Belgrade, while strolling the streets of Old Town, I had a curious encounter: I stumbled across a group of local bohemians. One of the men was a painter, whose father, a philosopher, had written a harsh critique of capitalism that begins with the following words (I received an English copy of the book, which I've had in my bag since last night): 'Dedicated to the North American Indians, the victims of the largest genocide in human history—committed by American capitalism.' As I was cutting the film, my mind kept wandering…

[The first time I held a 16mm camera was during my years as an art history student in Poland. I made one 16mm film with a friend who studied, albeit briefly, at the Lodz Film School, and we even got a mention at a student film festival in Germany. But these were now distant memories. Some years later, away from my duty as a jury member at the Batumi International Art House Film Festival in Georgia, I was pointing the camera, rather randomly, at various creatures, objects, and places. The rolls of film, as well as this 16mm non-reflex Bolex had been given to me by a close friend: 'Just play with it.' With this Bolex, and a bag filled with Yashica and out of date rolls of Super8 film purchased from American eBay, I strolled the streets of Batumi in search for my 'victims.' A number of years have passed, copious amounts of experimental films have been watched, and I still have not 'played' properly. I continued, although not-so-happily-any-more, to occupy the very safe borderland territory between having an idea and executing it. This decisive moment of picking up the camera and pressing the button… This was not to happen for a while. In recent years I have identified a potential programme of experimental filmmaking to enroll in, but financially speaking, it was not a viable option].

Back to the workshop. I stopped for a moment and looked around. Here they were: a group of local students of film and anthropology, two enthusiastic New Mexicans in charge, and curious members of the public: a man in his 70s, meticulously trying to put the frames of his film together with a splicer, and a local actor, who astonished everyone with his eccentric fur coat, which never came off his back. We were all in a state of temporary amusement. Which filmmaker said that to make films means to enter a child-like frame of mind? A certain state of always-ready-to-play and never-be-conscious-of-errors. 'Enthusiasm as the state of mind.' Never mind. The workshop came to an end and we looked at our films, combined by Michelle into one long loop, which she skillfully projected on a Steenbeck. 'Your film loops will be screened on the last night of the Festival,' we are told. 'How exciting,' I was thinking, even though I had scratched the letters on the surface of my strip the wrong way round, so they ended up projected backwards. That day I could not wait to return to my cozy hotel room. I was flooded with ideas for my future films. When revisited and confronted later, most of them, naturally, felt rather silly. But…the 'Hopi Film' is in the (slow) making. On a bus back to Old Belgrade, I was thinking how earlier that year, in a desperate need for a more stable academic position, I had applied for a number of post-doctoral fellowships all over the world. At that moment in Belgrade I began hoping that I would not get any of them (and I didn't). My mind was made up: I would enroll for an MFA in Filmmaking.

On Scorpios, Leather (and Satin) Jackets and the Importance of Experimental Film Festivals

[…]
10 December (Wednesday), 2014. Alternative Film and Video. Belgrade, Serbia.

In the Same Room (2014) is screening tonight at 21.00. I am curious how it feels to see one's film through other people's eyes. It is a privilege. I take a sip of whisky before entering the screening hall.

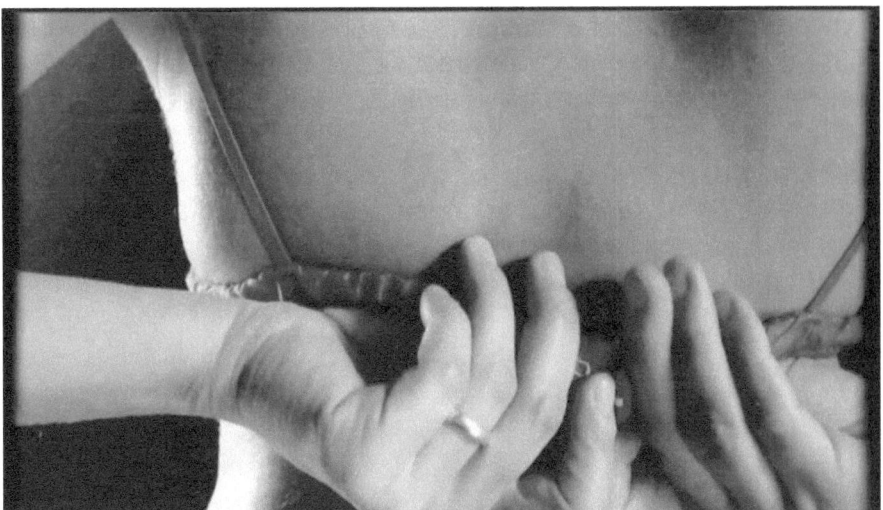

Still From *In the Same Room* (2014) By Kamila Kuc

P.S. The film that wins one of the mentions (and the residency at the dynamic Student Centre in Belgrade) at this year's Alternative Film/Video, Nina Kreuzinger's *Rettungsgriffe*, is one of the most exhilarating 16mm films I have seen in a long time. Plenty to learn, the journey continues. For certain, Alternative Film/Video is a filmmakers' and film lovers' festival.

****

On a less personal note…

Why attend experimental film festivals? And why are they important?

1.

In the first instance, it is important not only to have one's work screened, but also to see the work of others. The self-reflexive, critical nature of the avant-garde, to speak in Greenberg's terms, finds its reflection in experimental film festivals as the filmmakers continuously seek to redefine the discourse and nature of avant-garde filmmaking. In Foucault's terms, one can view these festival discourses as practices that 'form objects of which they speak.' Such discourses influence the ways in which ideas are then put back into practice. Such festivals are also educational. One often encounters the work that redefines our understanding of avant-garde film traditions. Such was the case with Bojana Vuyanovic's films, which I discovered at one of the Alternative Film/Video screenings in 2013. Being fairly familiar with the history of experimental film in Eastern Europe, and to some degree in the Balkans, it surprised me how little is still known about the formalist, structuralist-materialist tendencies in this region of Europe.

2.

Functioning as networking hubs, festival film screenings are surrounded by adrenaline-driven rituals. They also offer the most important form of non-monetary capital in the art world: having one's work seen by others prevents it from a second, 'spiritual death,' as Bazin would argue. Viewed in the screening room, the work is seen and recorded as being seen, thus it is forever imbedded in the viewers' collective memory (as well as in the festival catalogue, on various blogs and websites). This non-monetary capital can transform itself into a variety of future professional and personal opportunities, be it an invitation to another screening or event, or simply result in making new, likeminded friends.

On Scorpios, Leather (and Satin) Jackets and the Importance of Experimental Film Festivals

3.

But I am interested here in another factor that makes experimental film festivals important: ways in which the avant-garde infiltrates the mainstream and art cinema. An example: in Nicolas Winding Refn's highly celebrated 'art house blockbuster' *Drive* (2011), its main character, referred to as "Driver" (Ryan Gosling), wears a quilted satin jacket with a stitched scorpion at the back (now perfectly marketed by Amazon as 'DRIVE SCORPION BOMBER HARRINGTON QUILTED SATIN JACKET HAVE GOLDEN SCORPIO AT BACKSIDE'). Like Sailor's (Nicolas Cage) leather jacket in David Lynch's *Wild at Heart* (1990), the scorpion jacket acts as a 'symbol of individuality' and a 'belief in personal freedom.' In Refn's words, the jacket also functions as homage to one of the most iconic examples of avant-garde film, naturally, here we have Kenneth Anger's *Scorpio Rising* (1964) in mind. (The slowness of *Drive*, as well as of Refn's other films, can certainly be compared to Anger's avant-garde masterpiece.) Among many other popular filmmakers, Alfred Hitchcock famously acknowledged the impact of such avant-garde classics as *Un Chien Andalou* (Buñuel and Dalí, 1929) *L'Age d'Or* (Buñuel, 1930), *Entr'acte* (Clair, 1924), *The Fall of the House of Usher* (Epstein, 1928) and *The Blood of a Poet* (Jean Cocteau, 1932) on his own work.

The relationship between the avant-garde and the mainstream are more productive than generally assumed. Before becoming an Oscar-winning filmmaker, Kathryn Bigelow was part of the experimental art world: she collaborated with Vito Acconci and Richard Serra, among others. Steven Soderberg's *Traffic* (2000) was shot with a hand-held camera (operated by Soderbergh himself, under the alias 'Peter Andrews') to honour the Danish avant-garde movement Dogme95. The abstract cinematic collages of the Canadian avant-garde filmmaker Arthur Lipsett are a known influence on George Lucas's work. Michelangelo Antonioni's *Zabriskie Point* (1970) was influenced by Andy Warhol's 25-hour-long *Four Stars* (1967).

The examination of the relationship between the avant-garde and the mainstream requires more careful attention, as one may want to also think of works such as Joseph Cornell's *Rose Hobart* (1936) made out of *East of Borneo* (George Melford, 1931)—a classical Hollywood film; or more recently, Martin Arnold's *Passage à l'Acte* (1993), which is made from Robert Mulligan's *To Kill a Mockingbird (*1962). After all, subverting the rules requires knowing them. The key to all of this is that the avant-garde, by its definition, pushes the boundaries of what's generally acceptable. In 2006, the Ann Arbour Film Festival (which features experimental films) was attacked for its offensive programme, which resulted in a sudden withdrawal of state funding. The festival took the case to court over First Amendment violations. I am pleased to say that it won. It is great to observe that what the avant-garde had risked decades ago has become mainstream now. Take, for example, *Sweet Movie* (1974) by controversial Serbian counter-cinema director, Dušan Makavejev. The film was banned in almost every country due to its scatological scenes, which involved Otto Muehl's infamous avant-garde performance group urinating on each other, vomiting, defecating and consuming their own excrement. In 2014 a growing presence of the scatological can be seen in mainstream TV dramas. For instance, in *Boss* (Farhad Safinia, 2011, USA) the mayor of Chicago Tom Kane (Kelsey Grammer) shows an obvious disregard for one of his opponents by facing him from 'a throne.' The mayor then ends a conversation by offering to shake the man's hand without washing his hands after defecating. In *Fargo* (Noah Hawley, 2014, USA), mysterious hit man Lorne Malvo (Billy Bob Thornton) is also shown talking to a man while 'taking a dump.' This transgressive nature of contemporary mainstream TV is no doubt indebted to the avant-garde.

With all this said, by featuring examples of experimental films from all over the world, by filmmakers of diverse backgrounds and generations, of different aesthetic sensibilities, film festivals play a crucial role in endorsing the avant-garde spirit of cutting-edge innovation. I am honoured to be a part of Experiments in Cinema this year, a creative venture that I was introduced to in Serbia, of all places…

I wish to offer my gratitude to Joanna Zylinska and Timothy Quay for their helpful comments on the final version of this piece.

About the Artist

Kamila Kuc, Ph.D., is a writer, experimental filmmaker and curator. She is currently an Assistant Professor in the Media and Communications Department at Goldsmiths, University of London. She publishes widely on the subject of experimental film. She has also curated programmes of experimental film for international film festivals and venues (New Horizons Film Festival, Poland; Cinephilia, UK; Experiments in Cinema, USA). Her short films have been screened most recently at at the Alternative Film/Video in Belgrade, Serbia (December 2014). Her latest collaborative project centres on co-curating and editing *Photomediations Open Book*, a creative multi-platform resource concerned with the dynamic relationship between photography and other media.

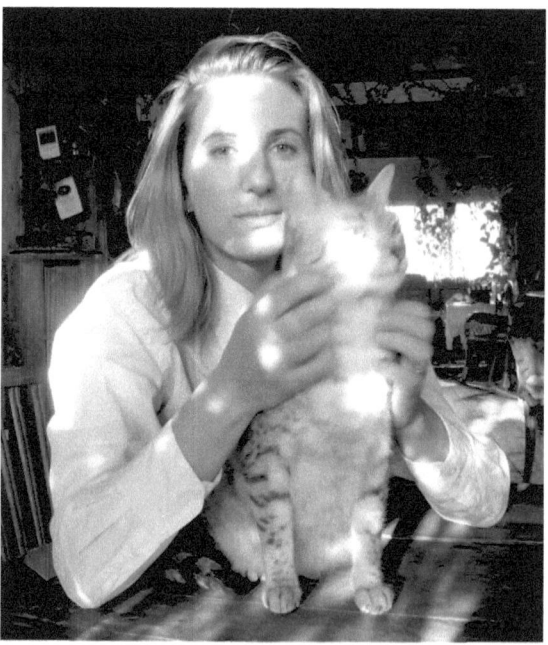

Portrait by Timothy Quay

on **CROSSROADS**

By: Steve Polta

San Francisco Cinematheque was founded in the summer of 1961 by filmmaker Bruce Baillie as a DIY venture (what we would now call a "microcinema") with a screening in his mother's front yard in the East Bay community of Canyon, California. Since this founding over five decades ago, Cinematheque has consistently exhibited non-mainstream works of artist-made cinema—known variously as avant-garde, experimental, personal, and underground. Based primarily in the city of San Francisco since the late 1960s, Cinematheque has undergone numerous transitions and staffing structures, has experimented with a variety of curatorial models and—not having a permanent home exhibition venue—has presented programs in virtually every conceivable type of venue, including parks and street corners; art galleries and bookstores; science and art museums[1], colleges and art schools[2] and storefront microcinema venues[3], as well as in unnamed artists' warehouses, and majestic movie palaces such as the Castro Theatre. The broad curatorial mandate of Cinematheque is to exhibit and celebrate non-commercial non-mainstream works of artist-made cinema (referred to often in shorthand form as "avant-garde" or "experimental" film and/or video) from all moments in its history and from as many geo-political locales as possible, to present canonical works as well as obscure and unknown works and to present works which confirm and challenge established film history and aesthetics. Each year, in the course of year-round programming, Cinematheque presents between 35 and 50 individual film/video screenings that include hundreds of individual works of artist-made cinema. Through these activities, Cinematheque has, over the years, supported the careers of literally thousands of film/video artists.[4]

I personally have been involved in non-mainstream film exhibition in the San Francisco Bay Area since January 1996. At this time I was in the Filmmaking MFA program at the San Francisco Art Institute and began assisting filmmaker Craig Baldwin (a professor of mine from my undergraduate days at UC Berkeley) in his ongoing curatorial project Other Cinema, something I would do consistently, thirty-six Saturdays a year, for the next seventeen years. In addition to this activity, I joined the staff of San Francisco Cinematheque in 1998 as a part-time office manager; I am currently the organization's Artistic Director and Archivist, positions I've held since 2008 (or thereabouts). In these years and through these two affiliations I've been involved with the presentation of over 1,000 non-mainstream film/video screenings.

Early in my time at Cinematheque I had proposed the idea of an annual festival. The general idea was to create an occasion, to form something of a concentrated focus, on contemporary film work primarily, but also on the activities of Cinematheque. It had seemed to me back then (and now actually) frustrating that, given Cinematheque's general persistent exhibition schedule (an average of one–three screenings weekly, nine months a year), our profile seemed to recede a bit into the general ambient cultural clutter of the San Francisco Bay Area.

Seeing how every little start-up festival (and the Bay Area has uncountable film festivals, large and small, representing every cultural niche and interest imaginable) seemed to draw attention, it seemed a strategic ploy to simply start up another one, a nice way to shed the proverbial light on our activities and the work of artists we screened. Also I'd felt, over the years, to varying degrees of chagrin, that Cinematheque was not as attentive or hip as it could be, was not as responsible to films and artists not already known to us, and that the curatorial approaches we'd been taking[5] simply did not include a mechanism for discovering new work and artists or an exciting format in which to screen such works. An annual festival—one which would deliberately seek new work—seemed to address these issues. And—strangely—while there were these myriad local festivals, there was not one dedicated to artist-made film of the "experimental" genres.

Thus it was that—after years of suggesting such a festival to a series of Cinematheque Directors and curators—Cinematheque's CROSSROADS film festival was conceived and established by myself, Jonathan Marlow and Vanessa O'Neill, then Cinematheque's Executive Director and Program Director, respectively, in 2009, with CROSSROADS' inaugural manifestation in May 2010. This festival has occurred annually since then.

The name of the festival—CROSSROADS—is an obvious reference to Bruce Conner's 1976 film of the same name. Following his death in mid-2008 and subsequent memorial screenings presented by Cinematheque at SFMOMA in 2009, Conner was much on our minds at the time of the festival's conception and early planning. The title was taken for the festival then not only in homage to this Bay Area icon but also as a way of suggesting the festival as a convergence of persons (audience, colleagues and artists) coming together from around the world to participate, meet and become inspired, and as a place for considering the juxtaposition of genres. There was of course the troubled, but appealing, metaphor in Conner's film of a beautiful explosion—which is also a history-changing event—sending silent infiltrating radiance across the globe. The name of the festival is properly expressed in all caps as a way of signaling permanence, gravity and longevity.

Since its conception, the "home venue" for CROSSROADS has been San Francisco's Victoria Theatre, your classic "moldering movie palace" type place[6]—family-run, with dysfunctional popcorn machine (sometimes it works; sometimes it doesn't) and classic (at times misspelled) marquee—with occasional programs held in additional venues.[7] For its first two years individual programs were autonomously curated by individual Cinematheque staff, in conversation with each other.[8] Since 2012, I have been the curator of CROSSROADS (in conversation with Cinematheque staff as well as with advisors and colleagues). Consistent supporters throughout the festival deserving of special attention include Kent Long and Vanessa O'Neill, who partner each year as the festival's technical directors; Cat Lam, the house projectionist at the Victoria Theatre and Christine Metropoulos—currently Cinematheque's Executive Director—who acted as CROSSROADS Festival Director 2012–14.

Films screened in CROSSROADS are drawn from works submitted in response to our annual call-for-entries, issued each year in the fall. In general these submissions are fascinating and, while at times the viewing process can be challenging, the variety and sheer weirdness of work that comes in is endlessly intriguing and inspiring, with the absolute best and most refreshing work coming soundly out of left field.[9] This pool of submissions is augmented with works viewed throughout the year in the course of curating seasonal programs, works viewed at collegial festivals or recommended by fellow curators. Relative to other film festivals, CROSSROADS' entry fees are deliberately low and waivers are frequently granted on request. Many filmmakers gladly pay entry fees as a way of supporting the festival and organization.[10] Entries are free for Cinematheque members. It is worth mentioning that Cinematheque limits CROSSROADS call-for-entries generally to our own website, email announcements and social media outlets with announcements made to the venerable Frameworks LISTSERV as well. The call-for-entries is deliberately confined to these narrow channels to avoid a sense of exploitation: it would be easy work and easy money to solicit work from every film school in the nation but—being the idealistic martyrs that we are—the cynicism involved

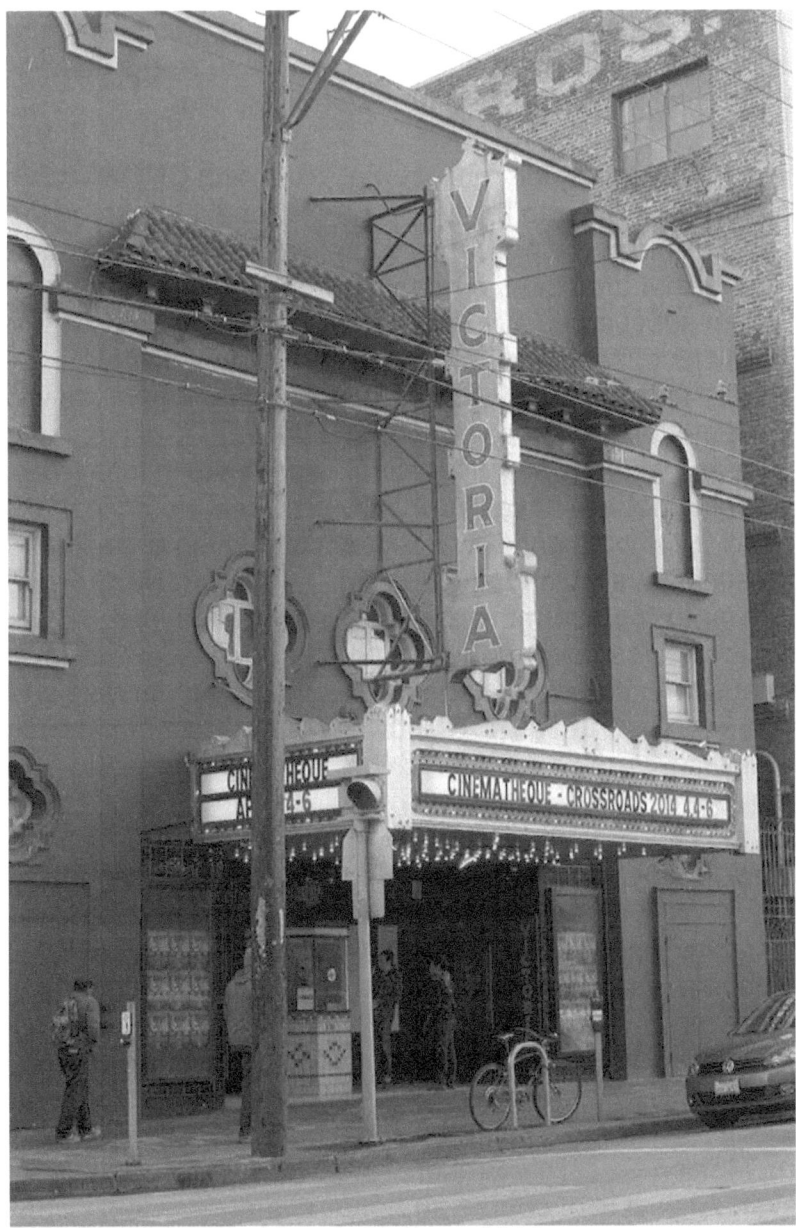

Victoria Theatre, 2014

in such outreach is beneath us. Of special note, Cinematheque pays rental fees for all works screened and honoraria to invited in-person guests. The primacy of payment to artists is a long-standing rule of Cinematheque and applies to works screened in the festival and throughout our screening year.

In terms of the curatorial philosophy governing CROSSROADS, nothing concerning the festival is set in stone. My personal belief, in terms of my passion for the field and my interests as a curator, is that the works emanating from experimental film/video subcultures—in their varied and combined explorations of sensuality and physicality, ir/rationality, language, artistic enunciation and speculative inquiry, as well as the varied experiences of time and the works' capacities to explore and express the diversity of experience in infinite and overlapping detail—have historically provided the richest, most complex, conflicted and rewarding accumulation of aesthetic experiences available in any art form. CROSSROADS seeks each year to represent this diversity, abundance and multiplicity. In complement to Cinematheque's non-festival presentation of historical and contemporary work and solo artist screenings, CROSSROADS showcases new work (generally created within two years prior to the call-for-entries) and operates under a general ethic of inclusivity. CROSSROADS includes not just works by known, canonized or "emerging" filmmakers but also works that might be uncertain, tentative or immature, works that might resonate in uncomfortable ways with mature work, works that might seem searching or questioning, as opposed to those making solid statements.

Major works—works which have gone on to acclaim and/or wide recognition—which have received their world premieres at CROSSROADS have included Jodie Mack's Dusty Stacks of Mom, Mónica Savirón's Broken Tongue and Scott Stark's The Realist. While it is of course an honor to premiere such films and see them achieve subsequent recognition, it is equally delightful to screen confounding works by lesser-known filmmakers in this context and to see these works subsequently infiltrate the world like mysteriously mutant creatures. Finally,

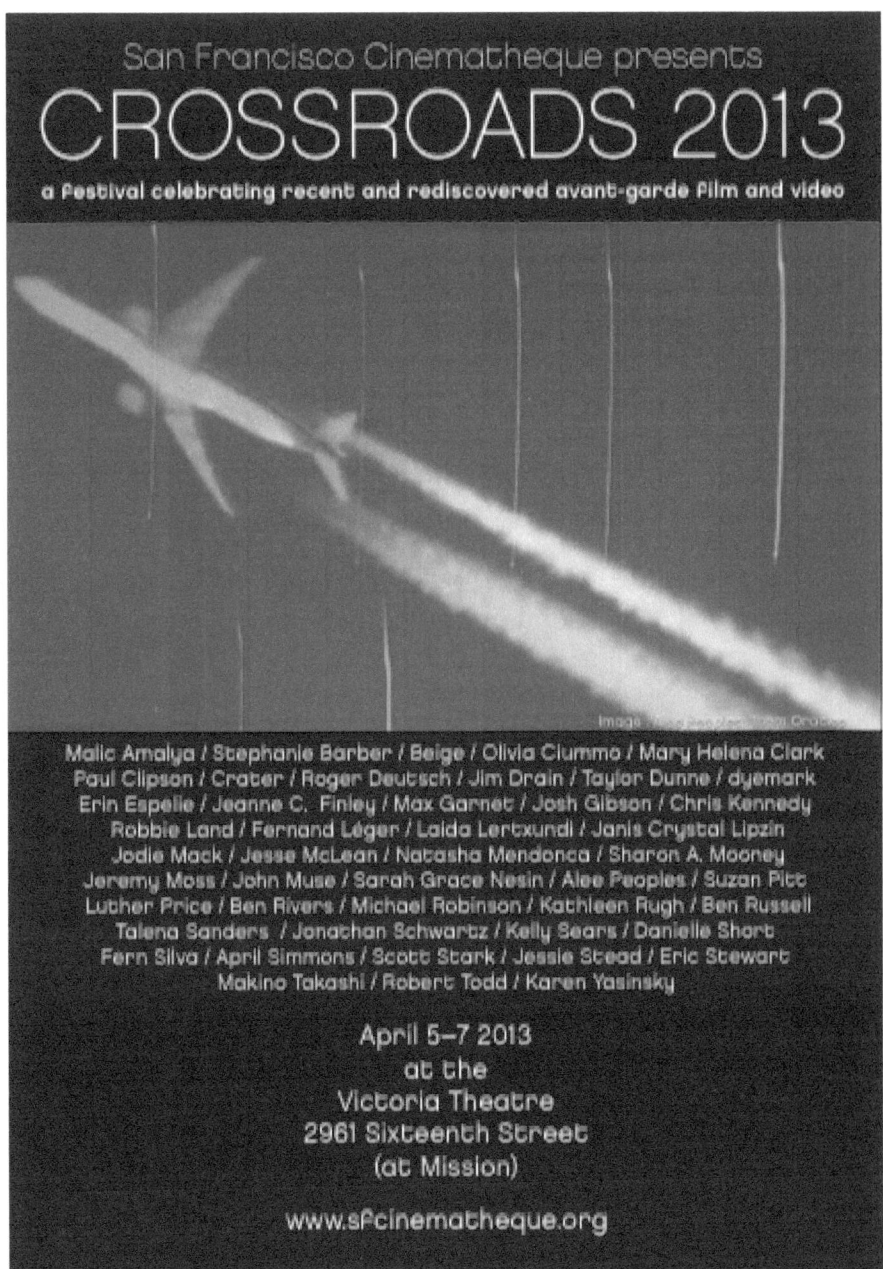

CROSSROADS seeks to be international in scope while remaining responsible and inspiring to local audiences and (most importantly) artists.

Each year since 2011 (the second year of the festival), CROSSROADS has featured as its centerpiece a program known as Apparent Motion, an extremely popular program of contemporary performance cinema. These have included multi-projector "expanded cinema" performances, live sound/image hybrid works and video improvisations. Featured artists in this series have included Kenneth Atchley, Elise Baldwin, Kerry Laitala & John Davis and Greg Pope as well as the collaborative performance groups Beige, Crater and MSHR, among others.[11]

In general, the bulk of CROSSROADS programs consist of groupings of films in resonant arrangements. Obviously (if you ask me) this is what all film curating should reach for. Such organizing principles are often more or less intuitive, associational and are frequently (and intentionally) left vague under a perhaps suggestive program title, one that is hopefully evocative and potentially serendipitously discoverable. For example, the program ...for there our captors demanded songs of joy[12] assembles films which—to me—feel like strangely satisfied end-times films, films made comfortably by the last person alive, suggesting themes of vague captivity in oddly expansive confinement. phantom tunneling 2: life is long, the walls come off, and light enters your cell(s)[13] is an uncomfortable program concerning voyeurism and spectatorship, institutional cruelty, the panoptic state and the depiction of human bodies on screen. It is worth noting that—while obviously reflecting (more or less) the curator's (i.e., my) personal concerns and interests—these themes emerge from suggestions discovered in viewing the films themselves. Experience has proven that forcing films into service of imposed ideas does not generally ring true and can be a disservice to the works. In any case, it's difficult and perhaps

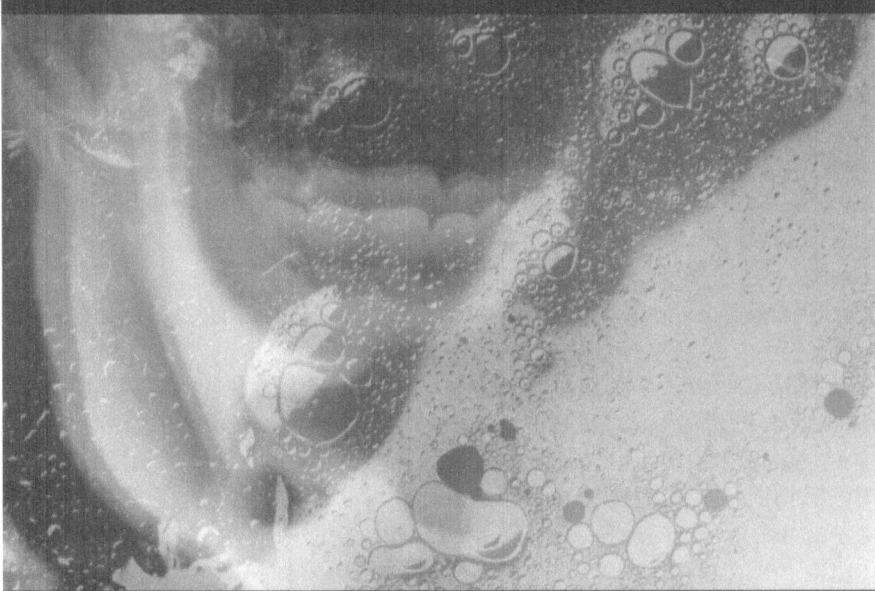

counter-productive to be too overt and literal in elaborating these inter-filmic resonances. There is value, after all, in confusion.[14]

Each expression of CROSSROADS is a continuation and a growth, but each is, hopefully, it's own thing and, hopefully, a complicated and rich experience for those who view it in its entirety. As the sixth iteration approaches (April 10–12, 2015), CROSSROADS feels to be evolving from infancy to something resembling a striving and resolute adolescence. After five years—with no overarching institutional support or reliably dedicated funding stream—we are finally figuring out what we are doing. Thanks in large part to CROSSROADS, Cinematheque's scope—in terms of its international reach and position in relation to an international community of artists and collegial institutions—is more expansive than it has ever been. Moving, thrilling, confusing and challenging non-commercial and experimental film/video work is being created at a scale that is unprecedented and, in my opinion, exciting. The establishment of CROSSROADS has without a doubt been a huge source of personal and professional pride and high point in my so-called career in non-profit, non-commercial ("artist-made") film exhibition. The big expression of gratitude of course goes to all the wonderful filmmakers, contemporary and historic, whose constant work—work done, essentially, for sake of community, personal expression, artistic dialog—has contributed to the present moment of prolific (if tenuous) artistic abundance. It is out of dedication to this community that Cinematheque and CROSSROADS emerged and it is why we continue to exist.

— Steve Polta. Mudrakers Café, Berkeley CA. December 2014.

About the Artist

Steve Polta is a filmmaker, curator/arts admisistrator, sometimes sound artist, occasional writer and occasional historian living in the San Francisco Bay Area. Steve Polta is Artistic Director/Archivist of San Francisco Cinematheque and curator of the annual CROSSROADS film festival. He holds a BA in Film Studies from UC Berkeley, an MFA in Filmmaking from the San Francisco Art Institute, and a Masters of Library and Information Science (MLIS) degree from San Jose State University. As a filmmaker, he has presented solo programs of his films at such venues Anthology Film Archives, Chicago Filmmakers and San Francisco Cinematheque and has been included in film programs presented at the Museums of Modern Art (New York and San Francisco), the New York Film Festival, the Pacific Film Archive and other venues. He was a programming associate of Craig Baldwin's Other Cinema since 1996–2013. Historical articles and interviews by him have been published recently in/on *Eat/Drink/Film, INCITE!, Radical Light* and elsewhere. He can occasionally be heard as a radio DJ on KALX Berkeley under a cryptic pseudonym.

References

[1] including the Exploratorium, the San Francisco Museum of Modern Art and Yerba Buena Center for the Arts.
[2] most notably a thirty-year run at the San Francisco Art Institute 1971–2001.
[3] such as Artists' Television Access.
[4] Additionally, Cinematheque creates publications and online resources \documenting the field of artist-made film and video and maintains an important historical research archive of published and unpublished materials that informs scholarly and curatorial research.
[5] Remember this was before the internet!
[6] which of course was known for porn exhibition in the 1970s.

[7]CROSSROADS 2011—Cinematheque's 50th Anniversary year—opened with *Radical Light: Cinematheque at 50*, a program celebrating this milestone (as well as the publication of *Radical Light: Alternative Film & Video in the San Francisco Bay Area* (Steve Anker, Kathy Geritz and Steve Seid, eds.), presented at SFMOMA. CROSSROADS 2014 opened with *Nathaniel Dorsky: Three Premieres*, screened at Yerba Buena Center for the Arts and also included Ben Rivers and Ben Russell's *A Spell to Ward Off the Darkness* presented as a spatialized installation at the Kadist Art Foundation.

[8]CROSSROADS 2010 included programs curated by Jonathan Marlow, Vanessa O'Neill and myself. 2011 saw programs curated by Marlow, myself and short-term staff member Lauren Sorenson.

[9]An absolute favorite film of mine—screened in CROSSROADS 2011—was Alee Peoples' *Boys of Summer*, a cracked and conspiratorial look at mythological male bonding subcultures extending back to biblical times, featuring Phil Collins and Don Henley, skater boys and ice cream. First viewing of this film (which was mailed in sans explanation on a DVD wrapped only in a xeroxed club flier depicting a screaming Little Richard) immediately suggested an attitude toward life and culture (pop and sub) completely different from anything else submitted; clearly an act of desperation, the film was so left field as to have been completely unpredictable. Similar random encounters with unpredictable filmic weirdness and/or unorthodox brilliance received via cold-submission (and which were new to Cinematheque) include the kaleidoscopic Marxist porno *Awe Shocks* by Anja Dornieden and Juan David González Monroy (screened 2012) and Alexander Stewart's post-apocalypse museum piece, *Crusts* (screened 2012) as well as the unique and emergent bodies of work shared by Olivia Ciummo, Christine Lucy Latimer and Jeremy Moss, to give just several examples of new-to-Cinematheque filmmakers first encountered via CROSSROADS.

[10] We know this because they tell us.

[11]Multi-projector works are also included as a matter of course

in general festival programming. Examples of this have been Christopher Harris' *28.IV.81 (Descending Figures)*, screened 2011; Jeanne Liotta's *Affect Theory*, screened 2014; and Scott Stark and Allison Leigh Holt's *Nocturnal Symmetries*, screened 2014. Additionally, a precedent for this centerpiece feature was the presentation of Stephanie Barber's live video performance *In the Jungle* as part of CROSSROADS 2010.

[12]CROSSROADS 2012. Complete program: *Man Is Always on the Stairs Between the Pleats of Matter and the Fields of the Soul* (2011) by Jing Niu; *L'eau, l'air et les songes (Water, air and dreams)* (2009) by Cécile Ravel and Jean-Marc Manteau; *Their Bird* (2010) and *A Child Goes Burying Dead Insects* (2009) by Rei Hayama; *Crusts* (2011) by Alexander Stewart; *Last Time* (2011) by Julia Shirar; *Light Licks: By the Waters of Babylon: This May Be the Last Time* (2011) by Saul Levine. www.sfcinematheque.org/crossroads2012_p6/

[13]CROSSROADS 2014. Complete program: *Quantum Tunneling* (2013) by Kadet Kuhne; *Drain* (2012) by Bettina Hoffmann; *The Blue Record* (2013) by Erik Anderson and Jeremy Moss; *Service of the Goods* (2013) by Jean-Paul Kelly; *The Lonely Life of Debby Adams* (2013) by Karen Yasinsky. www.sfcinematheque.org/screenings/crossroads-2014-program-10/

[14]A review of CROSSROADS 2014 which seems to understand and address this attitude and nicely discusses the above-discussed ethic of inclusivity is Michael Sicinski's "A Blistering Light at CROSSROADS Film Festival" which describes the festival as including "the untested, unknown, misunderstandable and inscrutable [...] nestled alongside obvious mastery." Also: "...it's when something knocks the hell out of us that we understand that something new is afoot, that things are changing, and that new art forms are pounding our minds into interesting new shapes." www.fandor.com/keyframe/a-blistering-light-at-crossroads-film-festival

Fracking (with) post-modernism, or there's a lil' Dr Frankenstein in all of us

By: Bryan Konefsky

Since the dawn of (wo)mankind we humans have had the keen, pro-cinematic ability to assess our surroundings in ways not unlike the quick, rack focus of a movie camera. We move fluidly between close examination (a form of deconstruction) to a wide-angle view of the world (contextualizing the minutiae of our dailiness within deep philosophical inquiries about the nature of existence). To this end, one could easily infer that Dziga Vertov's kino-eye might be a natural outgrowth of human evolution.

However, we should be mindful of obvious and impetuous conclusions that seem to lead – superficially – to the necessity of a kino-prosthesis. In terms of a kino-prosthesis, the discomfort associated with a camera-less experience is understood, especially in a world where, as articulated so well by thinkers such as Sherry Turkle or Marita Sturken, one impulsively records information as proof of experience (see Turkle's Alone Together: Why We Expect More From Technology and Less From Each Other and Sturken's Practices of Looking: An Introduction to Visual Culture).

The unsettling nature of a camera-less experience reminds me of visionary poet Lisa Gill (see her text Caput Nili), who once told me about a dream in which she and Orson Welles made a movie. The problem was that neither of them had a camera. Lisa is quick on her feet so her solution was simply to carve the movie into her arm. For Lisa, it is clear what the relationship is between a sharp blade and a camera, and the association abounds with metaphors and allusions to my understanding of the pro-cinematic human.

Fracking (with) post-modernism, or there's a lil' Dr Frankenstein in all of us

To dig a bit deeper into this notion of the pro-cinematic human, let us take a pop-culture leap and consider Herman Munster. Herman was a character from *The Munsters*, a popular American television comedy from the 1960s. This television show studied otherness using, as a filter, a mash-up of references to Universal Studios monster movies from the 1930s. In an episode from the 1965 season titled 'Will Success Spoil Herman Munster?', Herman performed a traditional American spiritual to express his particular understanding of experience. For Herman no camera was required – an acoustic guitar and the sincerity of his vocalizing were all that was necessary to reconstruct his meaty and visceral origins (see a clip from this episode at http://www.youtube.com/watch?v=MEpwnRsoj-s).

The song that Herman Munster sang is a traditional spiritual titled 'Dem' Dry Bones' written by James Weldon Johnson. Johnson composed this spiritual in the waning moments of the 19th century, about the same time that cinema was first invented (see http://everything2.com/title/Dem+Bones for the original song lyrics to 'Dem' Dry Bones'). Johnson was a civil rights activist, a songwriter, and the first African-American professor at New York University. 'Dem' Dry Bones' poetically explores a Christian sense of rapture and redemption. The suggestion is that in the after-life our sketetal remains will be miraculously reanimated by God (or Victor Frankenstein – we do not get to choose).

In my youth, the aphorism 'they are trying to playing God' was used in reference to either Prometheus or Mary Shelley's interpretation of that same mythological Greek character which took the form of the scientist Victor Frankenstein and his proto-steam-punk attempts to create life. Perhaps the functioning of a camera is more closely aligned with Victor Frankenstein's attempts to play God than what we might first imagine. Using a camera we paste together disparate pieces of information to construct a semblance of experience, and what emerges is a perverse expression of that which has been resurrected through the power and tyranny of the camera. Taking this notion of re-animation from the camera to the movie theatre, I am immediately reminded of Stanley Cavell's assertion that 'film is the medium of visible absence' (from his essay 'Psychoanalysis and Cinema'). The liminality of the screen gives us that which is simultaneously present and absent – nothing less than the undead. However, to be more exact within the context of this discussion, cinematic projection is in fact a projection of our imagination and fantasies stitched together to underscore the constructed nature of identity in ways that would make Victor Frankenstein proud.

Let us take a moment to step back from this kind of sutured specificity and consider a cinematic experience within a larger context. Our first step might be an assertion that art is an inherently human activity; keep in mind of course that in this age of the cyborg defining 'human' is becoming slippery. Art, at least for the moment, gives us a valuable barometric read of the human condition, a powerful mirroring of the self both individually and collectively. The next step might be to consider the potential meta-ness of cinema. Like opera, cinema is unique in that it has the possibility of containing so many of the other arts (music in a soundtrack, painting in composing one's image, theater in terms of the meat-puppets we might employ, etc.). Therefore, one could conclude that if art has a responsibility to give us an accurate, barometric read of the human condition then cinema (as a meta art form) has a particularly unique responsibility in this regard. Perhaps this is why we believe so strongly in the imagination of the kino-eye, even though Susan Sontag in her essay 'On Photography' cautioned against such zealous and non-critical views of all things mediated.

Fracking (with) post-modernism, or there's a lil' Dr Frankenstein in all of us

To exemplify this zealousness one might recall that when photography was first invented there were Congressional debates in the United States as to whether or not a photograph can, in fact, steal one's soul. I would argue that those debates were the last time the U.S. Congress discussed anything of intellectual value. Of course these days the Monsanto Corporation (probably with Congressional support) has soul-stealing wrapped up in the grizzly and disturbing form of GMO-modified DNA.

However, there does exist a cultural escape route, if one finds one's way to the writings of media theorist Gene Youngblood. Youngblood writes that we have the ability to turn off our attraction to mainstream nonsense and secede from the broadcast as a way of simultaneously retreating from one's addiction to consumer media and emerging into new, participatory, autonomous reality communities (see http://www.secessionfromthebroadcast.org/). According to Youngblood, there is a value to media fragmentation located (predictably) in the 'wild and wooly' World Wide Web. Although the seemingly endless possibilities of online media options diminishes the naively utopic dreams of past generations, current technologies give us the opportunity to weave together and, most importantly, share with others media worlds (autonomous reality communities) of our own design.

The possibility of employing new technologies to craft individual but inter-connected realities is something that could only be imagined just a short time ago. Think about the autonomous reality communities modeled by artists Sherrie Rabinowitz and Kit Galloway through their telecommunications research in the 1970s and 1980s (quite a few years before the Internet). This research resulted in such projects as 'Hole in Space', or their dream of global Electronic Cafes where people might communicate with each other in real time, on a real scale (with sound and image), in environments whose sense of presence

Youngblood calls 'emotional bandwidth' (see http://www.ecafe.com/getty/HIS/ for more information about Rabinowitz and Galloway's work).

Unfortunately, autonomous reality communities are often consumer-driven, as Michel Maffesoli studied in his text *Time of the Tribes: The Decline of Individualism in Mass Society*. Consider the proliferation of tribalized situations wrestled away from survival or biological imperatives. For example, we might wake in the morning and, dressed in our exercise outfit, find ourselves to be a member of the tribe of Nike. Later in the day we then find ourselves in a coffee shop, now a member of the tribe of Starbucks. When the workday ends we might find ourselves heading home encased in the petrol-driven tribe of Honda, Volkswagen, or Chevrolet. It is important to remember that these capital-driven tribes exist at the ass-end of the promise of Youngblood's participatory, emotional bandwidth. However, in spite of the multitude of fractured, consumer-based tribes that lure us with the promise of 'more', it is still possible to glean value and a sense of self from these somewhat misguided, market-driven communities. In other words, like heat-seeking missiles we hunger for 'story' – and for better or worse, we always find it.

Let us come back to our previously discussed pro-cinematic ability to simultaneously assess the micro and the macro in our surroundings. To this end consider Werner Herzog's film *Cave of Forgotten Dreams* (2010). Think of the many (disembodied) hands drawn on the prehistoric cave walls in that movie. Think about how the specificity of that 'I was here' gesture was paired with other carved images suggesting the grand narratives of history ('this is WHY I was here'). Also, think about how these stone carvings might not exist far from Lisa Gill's violent gesture of a movie etched onto her own body with a sharp blade. Additionally, let us not forget the underlying sense of

'why I was here' poetically expressed in the song 'Dem' Dry
Bones'.

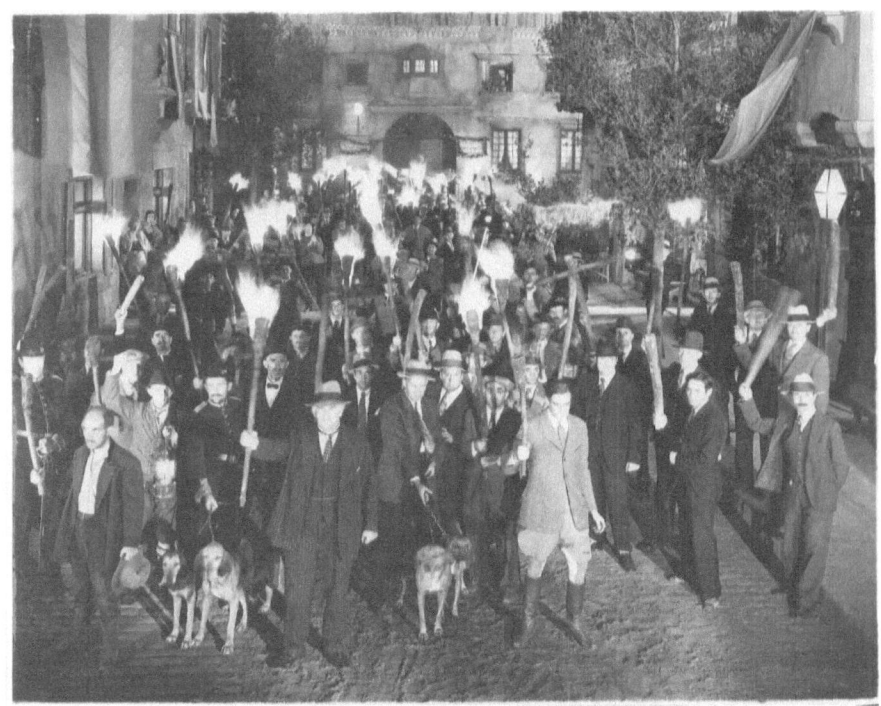

Still from *Frankenstein* (1931) By James Whale

Do know that I am mindful about invoking the 'grand narratives
of history' in these post-historic times. However, the moment is
ripe to pause on Carl Becker's 'pre-' post-historic essay from
1935 titled 'Everyman, His Own Historian'. In this essay Becker
rethinks the recording of history from a different perspective.
This rethinking prefigures American historian Howard Zinn's
life-long study of U.S. history from the perspective of the
country's most disenfranchised citizens (see Zinn's text *A
People's History of the United States*). For Becker (like Zinn
years later) we are each our own historic experts. The
specificity of our own stories and experiences are highly
individual yet necessarily connected. There is power in these
collective and collected individual voices.

Note how in *The Munsters* video clip Herman Munster sang (at the end of his cover version of 'Dem' Dry Bones') 'and that's how Hermie-baby was born!' Herman Munster celebrated his own personal story, understanding that his experience was also a meta-experience that was mnemonically contained within the many body parts from which he was sutured together. Herman's song was a comedic yet respectful nod to his maker – an expression of how profoundly Victor Frankenstein was invested in the storied consequences of collage, assemblage, and montage.

Approximately 75 years before the invention of the movie camera, and years before the pro-cinematic experiments of Étienne-Jules Marey and Eadweard Muybridge, Mary Shelley's novel *Frankenstein* explored the necessarily monstrous results of assemblage and montage. Note the sense of story and 'putting back together' that emerges in Victor Frankenstein's 'filthy workshop of creation' (as described by Judith Halberstam in her book *Skin Shows: Gothic Horror and the Technology* of *Monsters*), in spite of the grizzly protests from disparate muscles, glands, tissues, and organs. Frankenstein's scientific imaginings were not unlike what Catherine Russell described in her essay 'Archival Apocalypse' about found footage filmmaking. For her, this cinematic re-assemblage manifests itself as 'an aesthetic of ruins'.

The ruins of grand historic narratives might also be the sub-plot of Becker's essay 'Everyman His Own Historian'. For Becker, part of the unraveling of grand narratives involves each individual's sense of the 'specious present', a phrase that was first popularized by American philosopher William James in the 1800s. For James, this expression has to do with the elasticity of time and event – temporal illusions. These temporal illusions were first studied by James with the aide of chloral hydrate, amyl nitrite, nitrous oxide, and peyote.

Of course we cannot really escape time. James' 'rubber banding' of events is an interesting intellectual exercise but not something that is readily available to us. We can imagine and we can fantasize but, until the Zombie Apocalypse, time is inescapable. Never mind the a-historic claims of post-modernism. We are, in fact, always trapped in time. So, the idea of post-history, while an interesting idea, is undermined in the visceral, meat space of reality. Perhaps this is why a cinematic examination of human experience is so attractive – it is the one place (outside of death) where we can lose ourselves (momentarily) in the specious and elastic present of projected light. It is the place where we can time travel (whether through historic narratives, flashbacks, slow motion, or fast forward).

If this essay focused a bit more on the horror film genre we might explore, in greater detail, one of its basic tenets: the precariousness of human identity and how it can be lost or invaded (see Stephen Mulhall's essay 'Kane's Son, Cain's Daughter: Ridley Scott's Alien'). The suggestion here is that an essential sense of self is 'up for grabs'. What follows this loss of 'the essential' is improvisation. For me, that is where the fun begins. When we allow ourselves to transcend conventions cinema then becomes a wildly improvisational and instruction-less activity (perhaps with a little Promethean grand-standing thrown in).

Ultimately, improvisation is all we have. As author Kurt Vonnegut wrote in his book *A Man Without a Country*, '…we are here on earth to fart around, and don't let anybody tell you different'. This 'farting around' is, of course, a version of improvisation. In cinematic terms Vonnegut's 'farting around' suggests montage (the suturing together of the disparate bits and pieces). What often happens is that the 'putting back together' involves ruptures and mistakes that might parallel the re-contextualization experienced in found footage filmmaking. Again, we are talking about improvisation with, perhaps, a pinch of madness and monstrosity tossed in for good measure. Cinematically we are cross-threading a screw, we are insisting that the square peg WILL fit in the round hole, and we are 'throwing caution to the wind' just to see what story (or stories) might happen. The results of these improvised activities give us pause and an opportunity for reflection and invention.

Thinking deeper about Vonnegut's 'farting around', consider the root ideas of Gestalt psychology in terms of the holistic functioning of the human brain. We take things apart (in some cases with the aid of amyl nitrite or peyote) because it is in our nature to put them back together again (in one monstrous form or another). We simply cannot help ourselves.

Visionary film artist Stan Brakhage insisted that the true nature of cinema exists in the gutter-space between the frames. According to the ancient inhabitants of Herzog's movie *Cave of Forgotten Dreams*, the true nature of being lurks in the dark Platonic shadows of a cavern. Either way it seems that the 'pulling apart' and 'putting back together' cannot be separated. There is no isolated and autonomous moment of 'in-betweeness' as we begin to understand the physics of co-existence and mutuality.

Here I am thinking about a film titled *Splice Lines* (2012) made by the Canadian media artist Clint Enns. This short film is constructed using only the splice lines from Austrian filmmaker Kurt Kren's celebration of the human body titled *Mama und Papa* (1964). These splice lines represent the literal glue that holds Kren's shots together and metaphorically (maybe not unlike Brakhage's 'between the frames' assertion) suggest vast and expansive landscapes of the imagination. In Enns' film it is implied that Brakhage's 'gutter space' serves two functions. Yes, there is a world in there, but let us never forget that this world is also the glue that holds the rest in place, as tenuous as that adhesion might be.

Fracking (with) post-modernism, or there's a lil' Dr Frankenstein in all of us

As strained (and tenuous) as the relationship sometimes feels, it seems that un-dependent cinema's careful and studied examination of the human condition would suffer if it were not in conversation with more popular (and often uncomfortably saccharine sweet) re-constructions of experience that we have come to know as 'going to the movies'. At the risk of overusing analogies and metaphors we might liken this sense of discomfort with the perpetual state of decay that delineates the whole of the monster in Mary Shelley's gothic novel.

There is magic in this often strained experimental/popular dialogue, not unlike the illusionist who, before our very eyes, dramatically cuts his assistant in half with a saw and then, in the blink of an eye, returns the two halves to their original human form (a single narrative is collaged together from a sequential group of individual parts). One might go so far as to identify a valuable lesson within this failure – that is, a failure in the dissection and a failure in the deconstruction. Here, the failure might align itself with Vonnegut's notion of 'farting around'. In other words, take comfort in knowing that the whole always emerges triumphant through the narrative arc of this particular illusion. I mention this slight-of-hand performance hoping that it might evoke the inherent magic of cinema. There is a magic in movement, a magic in projected light and, taking things a step further, a magic in the monstrous liminality – all of which express the 'fun and games' that are possible within the medium of visible absence.

Consequently, one might infer that the true meaning of cinema is only revealed when 'it' is put back together. However, the putting back together only happens because of the all-important 'taking apart'. To this end, the un-dependents – 'the walla group' (as it is called in popular cinema) – must be vigilant and prepared. We must be ready at a moments notice to go proudly and defiantly into the world with fists raised high and our un-dependent/experimental torches, saws, and pitchforks ready to engage, eviscerate, and, from time to time, fart around as we chant 'walla, walla, walla'.

About the Author

Bryan Konefsky is a cultural worker dedicated to the advancement of un-dependent, experimental media arts through his work as moving image artist, teacher, lecturer and film festival director. Konefsky is the founder and director of Experiments in Cinema film festival and the president of Basement Films, one of the few remaining first generation micro-cinemas. Konefsky's creative work has been supported by granting organizations such as The Trust For Mutual Understanding, The National Endowment for the Arts, The National Endowment for the Humanities and the Banff Centre for the Arts. Bryan has lectured and screened his work internationally at venues such as Blinding Light Cinema in Vancouver, the Videoex Festival in Switzerland, the Erarta Museum for Contemporary Art in Russia, the Paris Underground Film Festival in France, Cinema Ritrovato in Italy, the Oslo Film Institute in Norway, the European Media Arts Festival in Germany, Dongguk Universtiy in Seoul, South Korea, and the Bienal de la Imagen en Movimiento in Buenos Aires.

References

Becker, Carl L. "Everyman His Own Historian." Everyman His Own Historian; Essays on History and Politics. New York: F.S. Crofts, 1935. N. pag. Print.

Cavell, Stanley. "Psychoanalysis and Cinema." Contesting Tears: The Hollywood Melodrama of the Unknown Woman. Chicago: U of Chicago, 1996. N. pag. Print.

Fracking (with) post-modernism, or there's a lil' Dr Frankenstein in all of us

Gill, Lisa. Caput Nili: How I Won the War and Lost My Taste for Oranges. Albuquerque, NM: West End, 2011. Print.

Halberstam, Judith. "Making Monsters: Mary Shelly's Frankenstein." Skin Shows: Gothic Horror and the Technology of Monsters. Durham: Duke UP, 1995. N. pag. Print.

Maffesoli, Michel. The Time of the Tribes: The Decline of Individualism in Mass Society. London: Sage, 1996. Print.

Mulhall, Stephen. "Kane's Son, Cain's Daughter: Ridley Scott's Alien." On Film. London: Routledge, 2002. N. pag. Print.

Russell, Catherine. "Archival Apocalypse." Experimental Ethnography. Durham, NC: Duke UP, 1999. N. pag. Print.

Shelly, Mary. Frankenstein / Mary Shelly. New York: Pyramid, 1957. Print.

Sontag, Susan. "On Photography." A Susan Sontag Reader. New York: Farrar, Straus, Giroux, 1982. N. pag. Print.
Sturken, Marita, and Lisa Cartwright. Practices of Looking: An Introduction to Visual Culture. Oxford ; New York: Oxford UP, 2001. Print.

Turkle, Sherry. Alone Together: Why We Expect More from Technology and Less from Each Other. N.p.: n.p., n.d. Print.

Vonnegut, Kurt, and Daniel Simon. "Now Then I Have Some Good News." A Man without a Country. New York: Seven Stories, 2005. N. pag. Print.

Zinn, Howard. A People's History of the United States: 1492-2001. N.p.: n.p., n.d. Print.

Curating Artists' Cinema

By: Caroline Koebel

As a maker of experimental film and artists' video, I am keenly aware of the contemporaneous need for the making of context and community, for creating the (meta-) conditions of the work's existence beyond the source of origin, its contemplation by others. "Audience" as an abstract concept is a fount of desire, integral to critical and aesthetic process, and the basis of a dialogical ontology of filmmaking.

In their devotion both to filmmaking and disseminating radical film art culture, American avant-garde mavericks Maya Deren and Jonas Mekas inspire next generations also to simultaneously make and curate. Gen Xers such as me find a home in cinema-as-counter-hegemonic-expressive-form after being weaned on punk and hardcore music subcultures. Such currents of influence exude DIY and DIWO ethos, the very spirit that sparks today's most vital actions in global artists' cinema.

Various forces, from Craig Baldwin and Other Cinema in San Francisco to M.M. Serra and Film-Makers' Cooperative in NYC (to name two beacons), manifest a quintessential communality bent on sharing the autonomy, radicalism, and love of alter-cinema. The late Helen Hill—from the collective guide to hand-processing *Recipes for Disaster: A Handcrafted Film Cookbooklet* she spearheaded through teaching filmmaking to a broad demographic to her body of exuberant cinema—continues as an animate presence in this world.

These advocates unite artists and audiences: a community of makers whose works excite, awe, provoke, inspire, and challenge, and a community of moving image art enthusiasts who feel an affirmation of self by partaking of a personal, poetic, experimental, and critical cinema without commercial cachet.

Especially since the reality of experimental film and artists' video, historically, has been at such loggerheads with capital, it's understandable that avant-garde cinema's artists and audiences would be in such symbiosis and typically exhibit merely faint boundaries, if any at all. To be audience of this cinema is to be irrevocably marked by it; to become part of it; to carry it with you as a secret not to divulge on the marketplace but, hopefully, to be whispered into unsuspecting yet receptive ears.

The Friendship State is a program of films and videos by Lyndsay Bloom, Jennifer Lane, Kelly Sears, Scott Stark, and me that I presented originally at Microscope Gallery in November 2012. Texas-based at the time with an upcoming return visit to NYC, I wanted to articulate more formally the dialog already shaping between other makers and me around the state (Austin, Houston, Marfa) and to explore the state's desirable traits (the motto of Texas is "friendship"). Following the Brooklyn premiere, the program toured to Austin Film Society, CineMarfa, and Peras de Olmo - Ars Continua in Buenos Aires.

For the Friendship State at Zeitgeist Multi-Disciplinary Arts Center Lyndsay and I road- tripped to New Orleans, where our gracious and loquacious hosts were utterly captivating in their storytelling prowess. An especially memorable portrait drawn by Rene Broussard, Zeitgeist Director, was of his friendship with Helen Hill. Each week at the farmer's market Helen would buy a crawfish and on the walk home release it into the water. The friends shared this ritual throughout Helen's pregnancy and sustained it once the baby was born.

Curator's Corner is a feature of the Aurora Picture Show website for which Curator Mary Magsamen selects an APS member to spotlight (and streams their work). Stumbling upon the phenomenal animations of Kelly Sears on the site resulted in my programming a solo screening in May 2012 for Experimental Response Cinema (ERC) in Austin. Just as Kelly makes use of indispensable critical and creative tools in her life as an explorer of (the edges of) cinema, she likewise brings intense focus and precision to logistics and consequently the in-person Austin event was a jewel to behold on all levels.

Her apt sense of physics (and of other areas of scientific inquiry) infuses her powers to make motion out of still parts with anything but static results. *The Drift* in particular conveys a sense of liberatory movement both on and off screen (I recall feeling that I too, like an astronaut, was floating in space). In the Q&A the artist talked about training her brain's "animation muscle" and the significance of this highly intentional neurological process to her cinema. The night was a bright example of experimental film's capacity to exercise viewer's muscles, or rather whole beings, in myriad and lasting ways.

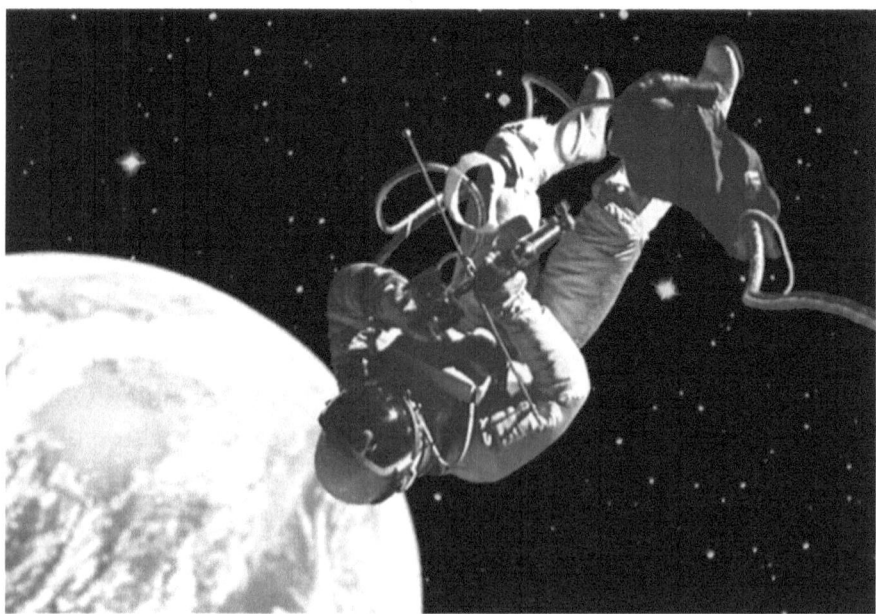

Still from *The Drift* (2007) By Kelly Sears

Commissioned by Aurora Picture Show, Kino B: Contemporary Cinema by Berlin-Based Artists premiered in October 2013 in Houston, Texas, and toured in 2014 to Transart Institute at Uferstudios in Berlin, Germany, and to the Wexner Center in Columbus, Ohio. Curatorial parameters entailed selecting an initial title from my base in Austin and then resisting any temptation for virtual research in favor of learning-in-place from a vantage point of Berlin itself (ultimately resulting in a frenzy of online communications and viewings and old-school meetings and real-live 16mm projections).

Thus, I landed in the foreign capital with Sylvia Schedelbauer's *Sounding Glass* in hand and a month later returned stateside with eight additional titles by the (now) late luminary Harun Farocki, Guillaume Cailleau & Ben Russell, Isabella Gresser, Bernd Lützeler, Anna Marziano, Deborah S. Phillips, Michael Poetschko, and Daniel Steegmann Mangrané—artists who share a command of cinema's potential for experientially transformative critical reflection.

It was a hot and humid August day in Berlin when I rode my bike east along Karl-Marx-Allee to the home studio of Harun Farocki and Antje Ehmann, passing the Computerspielemuseum on my way. Experiencing the pair in the intimacy of their own space has left a strong impression on me; the sight as we ranged over various topics and debated how different projects would resonate in the Kino B program of Harun drinking espresso and Antje eating an avocado remains vivid. The quiet yet palpable beauty of their bond gave me solace in the wake of the collapse of my own long-term relationship as I pedaled back west, passing once again the Computer Game Museum but now with the newly acquired knowledge that it, as a sponsor of Farocki's *Parallel*, would feature in my Kino B program.

In April 2013 I guest curated a special presentation for Fusebox Festival in Austin of *De Profundis*, a radical film experiment by Lawrence Brose inspired by Oscar Wilde's transgressive

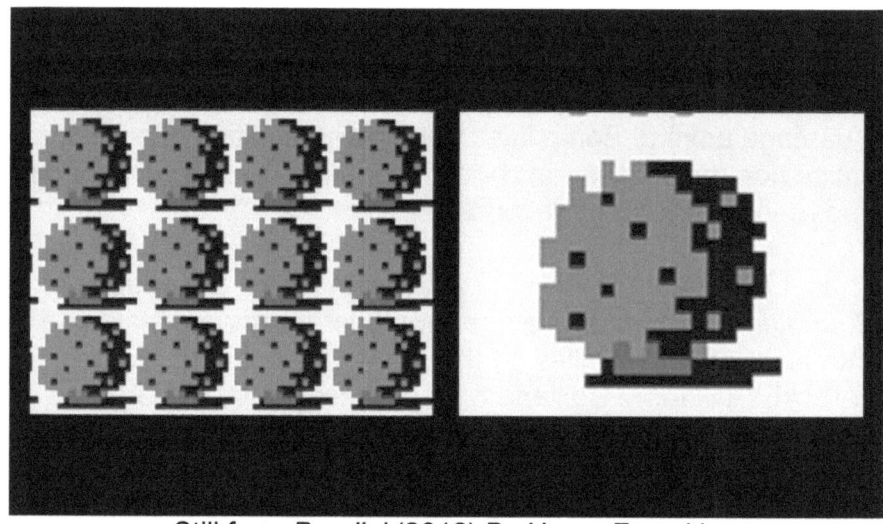

Still from *Parallel* (2012) By Harun Farocki

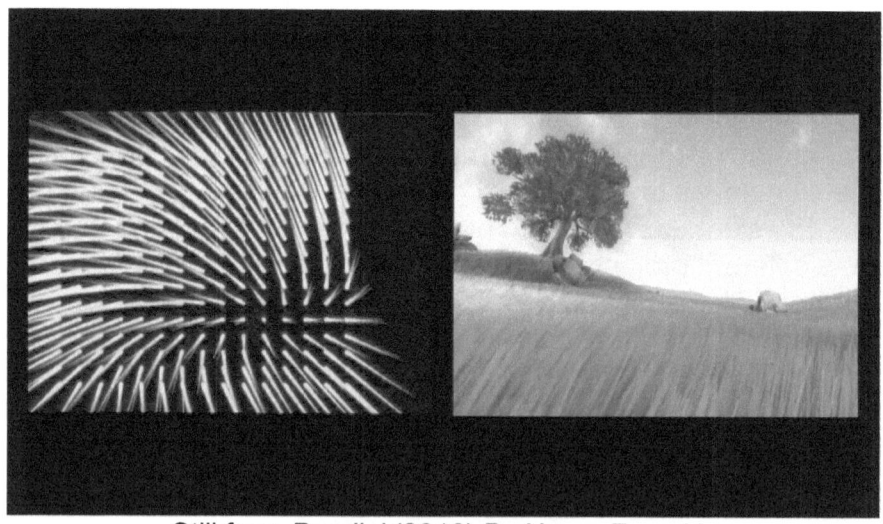

Still from *Parallel* (2012) By Harun Farocki

aesthetics and prison letter. Because at the time he himself was trapped in a legal battle, "The United States vs. Lawrence

Brose," the Buffalo-based filmmaker was prohibited from travel. Our initial work-around was to Skype him in live but due to additional legal restraints we screened a prerecorded video interview between Lawrence and William C. Altreuter, Attorney, addressing the 1997 film and Lawrence's current-day persecution in light of one another.

Yet for the artist's insight and prescience I'd like to turn to an earlier interview conducted by Scott MacDonald shortly after the release of *De Profundis*: "I did try to create a different kind of sonic space, and a sense of overload that would reflect our time and that earlier one. The arguments that were going on between Wilde and Gide, and between Wilde and the Victorian society that convicted him, are still going on. But a hundred years later, we've come to a position where, partly because of what happened around Wilde, we can have voices and even

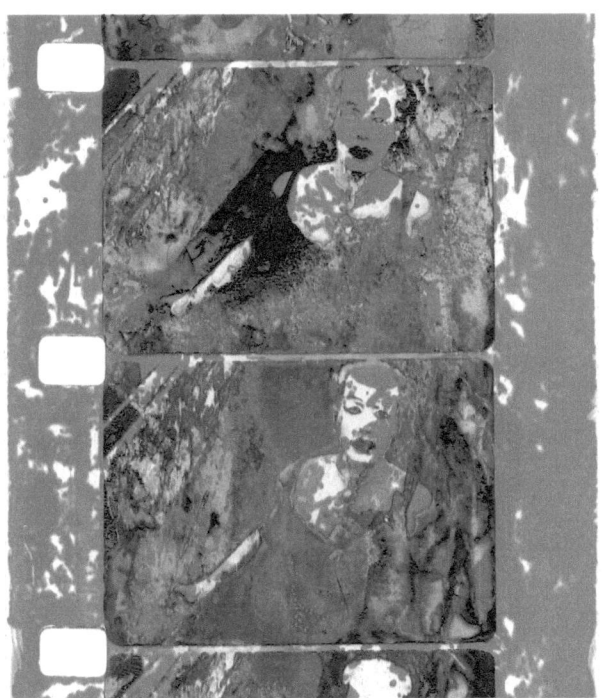

Still from *De Profundis* (1997) By Lawrence Brose

the beginnings of a language with which we can begin to discuss things. Yet language fails us."

I am returned here to curating artists' cinema. The crux of the matter is that an act of expression such as *De Profundis* wields immense powers of resistance to authoritarian structures and therefore is under constant peril of erasure (through various means of censorship and silencing). It is thrilling, affirming, and gratifying to coexist with others— significantly: artists and audiences—collectively maintaining that such cinema is not to be bullied out of existence.

About the Artist

Caroline Koebel makes experimental cinema clashing aesthetics and politics. Retrospectives include Festival Cine//B (Santiago), Centre for Contemporary Art at Ujazdowski Castle (Warsaw) and Directors Lounge (Berlin). She has presented at Experiments In Cinema (Albuquerque), Scope Art Fair (NYC), Edinburgh International Film Festival, European Media Art Festival (Osnabrück), LOOP Barcelona; published in *Brooklyn Rail*, *Afterimage*, *Jump Cut*, *Millennium Film Journal*. BA in Film Studies: UC Berkeley. MFA in Visual Arts: UC San Diego. She is on faculty at Transart Institute, and in summer 2015 will teach a Brecht Workshop in Berlin. Her solo show Incursions Into Cosmic Fear opens in June at Young Projects in Los Angeles.

Changing the World, One Film at a Time

By: Bart Weiss

First, I really need to say thank you to Bryan Konefsky and the great work that he's done creating and growing Experiments in Cinema. Every year that I've been to the festival, it's been an inspiring experience: the films, the audiences, the filmmakers, the workshops, and the community. I have made many friends through the festival, and look forward to making more. And I love the way he brings his students into the festival. It is truly a remarkable festival and a model for people who want to start their own festival. Thank you for your hard work, and your great smile.

So, a brief history of the Dallas VideoFest (Formally known as the Dallas Video Festival). In 1986, I co-hosted a program of video art from local and international filmmakers at the Dallas Museum of Art. It went way better than we expected. After the event, my friend John Held said, "That was fun, but I don't ever want to do that again." And for some unknown reason I said words that dramatically changed the course of my life,
"Well, let's have a festival, and we'll do it in four days."
And my friend Melissa Berry, who is in charge of programs at the Dallas Museum of Art, said,
"Okay."
Of course I had no idea what that meant.
Or how to get a video projector.
Or how to get programs.
Or an audience.
But I quickly found out.

So, we started in 1987.

The first program was Edie Adams presenting the work of Ernie Kovacs (the first artist to work in television), a program that set a perspective for the festival.

Over the years, several trends emerged as DVF found its identity.
A good dose of video art and experimental work of all kinds,
A large smattering of documentaries, not to be seen elsewhere in the region,
New kinds of dramatic work,
Some kind of interactive work,
Some kind of live video event,
And looking at what the possibilities of television could and should be.
We also heavily featured all kinds of work made about media and how it changes the world.

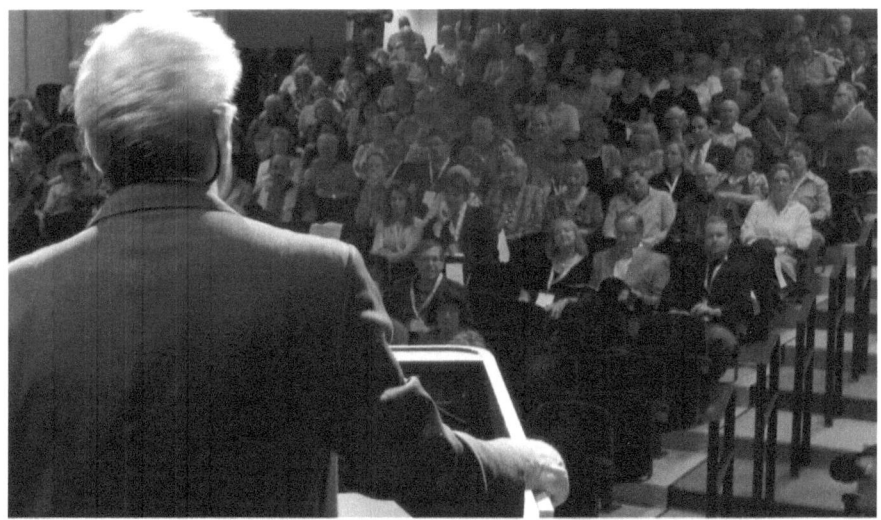

Bart Weiss—Dallas VideoFest 2012

Over the years, the amount of each has changed as my interests have shifted. (Or is it a reaction to the work that is out there, that had not been shown?)

We have showcased new technologies, not just to show them off, but to display how artists could work with mediums like video walls, high definition virtual reality (initially we had to get a deck shipped from Japan), CD-ROMs, interactive games, CD interactive, DVD, the Internet, transmedia and the Omni hotel wall in Dallas (with sound transmitted on KXT radio).

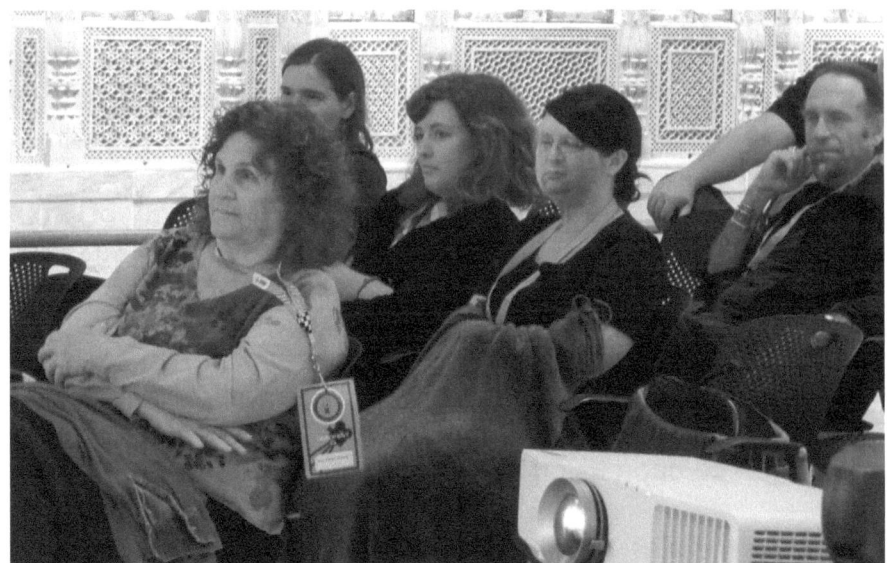

Bryan Konefsky with Michelle Mellor and Beth Hansen—Dallas VideoFest 2012

We also have led the way on how to use technology to run the festival: having early backend databases for entry, early use of video files to play back video, using Google Hangouts to do Q and A's before the fest, and other ways to help make our very small staff more productive.

Back in 1987 when we started the festival, there was only one other festival in town, so we felt we had a responsibility to show work in many sectors that were not at all served by that festival: African American, Latino, Gay and Lesbian, Asian, Jewish, and work by women. Since then, we have partnered with these sectors to create festivals specializing and serving their communities, and we showcase work from each in our larger festival each year.

So our role as a festival has changed, evolved, and morphed, although the core elements tend to be the same.

I tell my board that if we cannot fail, it is not worth doing. Each year, we try something we have not done. This year we commissioned a composer to do an original score to Hitchcock's The Lodger and had it performed by the Dallas Chamber Symphony. We also went from four days to five days and moved from two venues to five venues, but only have two programs at once. We also added an iPhone festival to the mix.

So why do we need a festival if you can see the history of moving images on YouTube? Well, do you remember the days of Blockbuster and going to a video store?

I would often watch people trying to decide what to go see. In a big store, people were frustrated. Too much choice! When everything is available to you at anytime, you tend not to see anything. The oppression of choice.

I firmly believe that people are affected by the images they consume. Most of the time when people walk away from the screen they say, "Boy, I'll never get those hours back." But there is lots of great inspiring media available for you, right at your fingertips; you just have to want to look.

My hope is that when you come to our festival and see the work I have selected, (or when you come to Experiments in Cinema) you will be inspired and you will not settle for the cat videos and zombie GIFs.

But there is more,
And that is about community. There is a community that comes to these festivals, that gathers for a series of days, gets inspired, commits to seeing each other later (and waits until next year to do that). But while we are there, we share that bond of cinema. We connect to the spirit that goes back to the history of cinema and further back to the history of storytelling. We gather and have a joint experience.

132

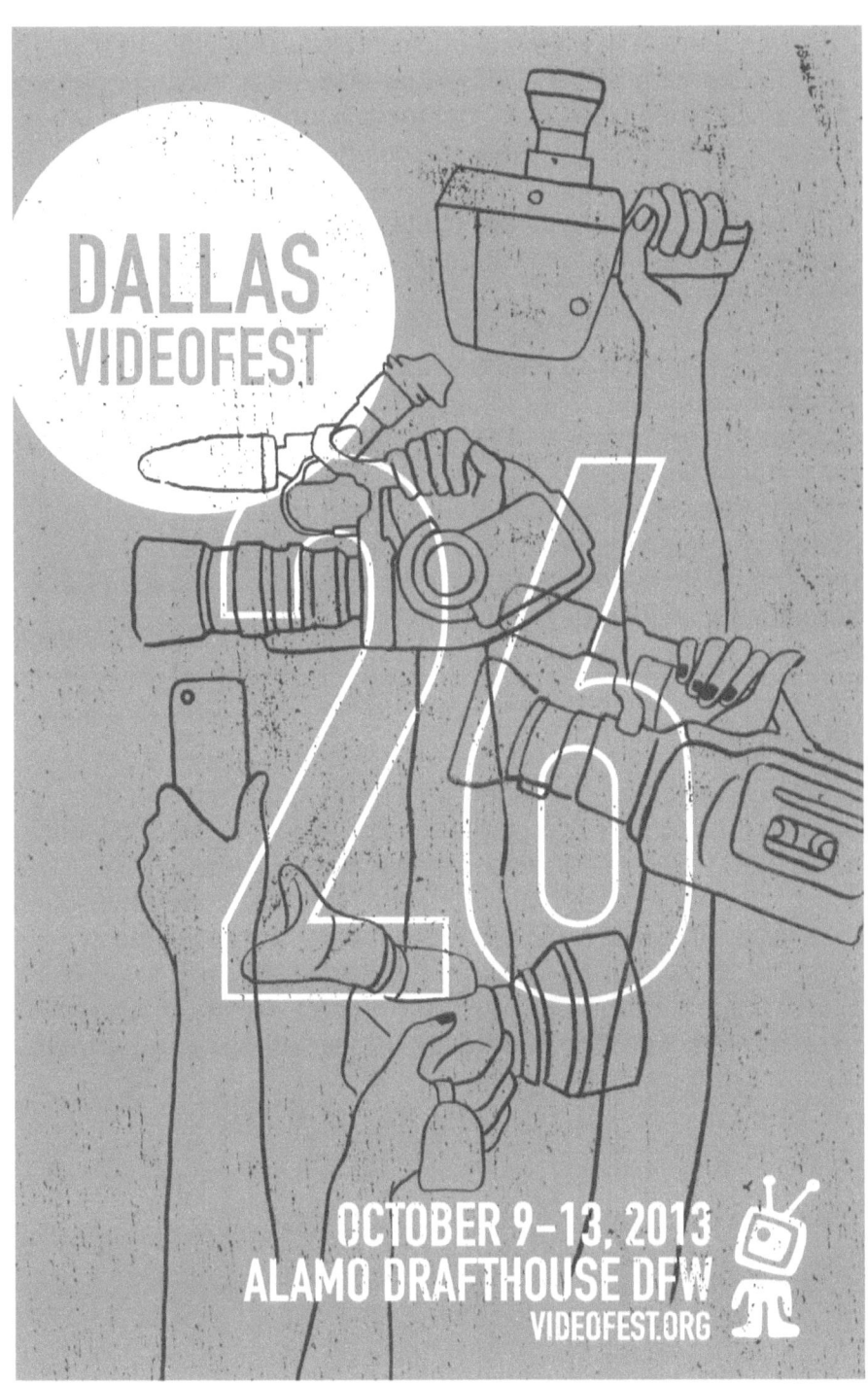

And then there is the filmmaker. As makers, we want to and need to experience the work with an audience. Having numbers on YouTube might be great, but there is nothing like being in the room when you can feel the audience getting the nuance that you spent hours and hours tweaking, and they experience it, and revel in it, and you are ecstatic. Without these connections between audience and makers, experimental work will not flourish.

In the overly saturated media world there is so much need for curators, compilers, taste shapers, connectors, friends, shamans, storytellers, and people who are so excited about the great possibility of what film can do. They will tell you to see this and see that, show it to you in a way that moves you, and makes you see your world in a completely different way. Or perhaps have a good laugh on a dark day, or be moved about something you never knew you needed to know.

About the Artist

Bart Weiss is an award-winning independent film and video producer, director, editor and educator, who has lived in Dallas since 1981. Bart is currently an Associate Professor at UT Arlington. He is mostly known as the director and founder of the Dallas VideoFest. He produces the TV show "Frame of Mind" on KERA TV in Dallas, and is the artistic Director of 3 Stars Cinema. He has traveled to Nigeria Pakistan and China to show American Documentaries for the US State Department.

Musings

Musings

www.ingramcontent.com/pod-product-compliance
Lightning Source LLC
Chambersburg PA
CBHW021954170526
45157CB00003B/984